MW01698679

TESTIMONIALS

"I felt a flood of emotions as I read this, happy because I didn't feel so alone in my fears, sad because I had lost so many I love, guilty because I am alive and healthy, worried that I might be next tomorrow, and a feeling of déjà vu with many of the experiences shared. I only hope and pray that [this book] can help other women who are as frightened as little girls when they ask, Am I next...?"

Bonnie S. • Texas, USA

"In the decade since the BRCA1 and BRCA2 genes were discovered, much has been written about the medical, scientific and legal issues raised by the discovery of these genes. In her book, ***Am I Next In Line?***, Monique Achtman writes candidly about the roller coaster experience of finding out that she is at high risk for breast and ovarian cancer. She explores deeply personal issues that many of us can identify with: fear, grief, loss, difficult decisions and painful choices. Monique tells her story with courage and honesty. Her book will raise awareness and stimulate public discussion about these important issues. Thank you, Monique, for sharing your journey with us."

Joanne Riediger-Duebel, President
Hereditary Breast & Ovarian Cancer Society of Alberta

"This book is a riveting personal journey into taking a proactive role in your health care. The story is poignant, uplifting and captures the emotional struggles and medical decisions faced by every woman who is told that she has a high risk for hereditary cancer. An important book with an important moral!"

Sue Friedman, DVM, Executive Director, FORCE:
Facing Our Risk of Cancer Empowered • Tampa, FL

"This is a fascinating book, well written, heartfelt, and courageous. As a person with a family history of breast cancer, I felt it raised issues I hadn't ever considered. It will be a helpful resource for many people: for those who have survived cancer, for those who have a family history of genetically transmitted diseases, and for those who are agonizing about BRCA gene testing."

Marilynne Lambert, MA, RSW • Bonnyville, Canada

"This is a truly remarkable and eminently readable account of your journey. I am sure that it will be very helpful to many people. It was a pleasure to meet you and read this journal."

Renée Martin, PhD, FCCMG, Medical Genetics • Calgary, Canada

"A smart, practical book from someone who's been there. Monique is generous with her insight into the personal and ethical issues surrounding gene testing and treatment. Part of the new breed of super-informed patients, Monique guides with hope and clear thinking through some of [her] life's most difficult, yet necessary choices."

Brian Cohen, B.A., LL.B, B.C.L. • Toronto, Canada

"...It is a wonderful, sincere sharing of a unique life experience. It should be of interest to a wide range of people – not just those who might share your situation, but to any who want to understand what it means to have to live close to cancer."

Ellis Bartkiewicz • Calgary, Canada

"I'm an hour into it and I just wanted to tell you this is very good!"

Debbie Elicksen • Calgary, Canada

"Congratulations on confronting your fears, investigating your family history and making an informed decision for your own health and peace of mind! I was thrown into this same journey through a diagnosis of breast cancer. My family physician referred me for genetic counseling as there is a very strong pattern of cancer, particularly breast cancer, in my family. I am currently awaiting gene test results so that I can make proactive decisions for my own health and inform my children and extended family for their protection. I admire your candor and openness in writing this book for others to share."

Leslie Choquette, Breast Cancer Survivor • Calgary, Canada

"Monique Achtman, a loving wife and mother in the prime of her life, was faced with the decisions to have BRCA gene testing and prophylactic surgery to remove, as she puts it, much of what physically made her a woman. With courage and candor, she shares her story in these pages in the hope that others at risk for hereditary breast and ovarian cancer will find peace of mind as they examine their options."

Warren Harbeck, Ph.D. • Cochrane, Canada

Am I Next In Line?

Am I Next In Line?

How I Conquered My Fear of
Hereditary Breast and Ovarian Cancer

A Personal Journey

Monique Achtman

Foreword by:

Dr. Rhiannon M. Hughes, MD, MSc, FRCPC, FCCMG
Assistant Professor, Departments of Oncology and Medical Genetics, University of Calgary

Am I Next In Line?

Notice of Rights

Notice of Liability

Credits

Cover: Paul Lambert and Myron B. Achtman

Design: Myron B. Achtman, adita@adita.com

Substantive editing: Julie Black, JulieBlack@shaw.ca

Library and Archives Canada Cataloguing in Publication

Achtman, Monique, 1965-

Am I next in line? : how I conquered my fear of hereditary breast and ovarian cancer : a personal journey / Monique Achtman.

ISBN 0-9733732-0-2

1. Cancer—Genetic aspects. 2. Achtman, Monique, 1965- —Health. 3. Breast—Cancer—Genetic aspects. 4. Ovaries—Cancer—Genetic aspects. 5. Genetic counseling. I. Title.

RC268.48.A24 2004 616.99'449042'092 C2004-906738-9

Printed and bound in Canada.

DEDICATION

This book is written for my children and the reader, who, like them, has a family history riddled with early cancer diagnosis and who wants to do everything within reason to create a program of increased cancer surveillance and prevention.

In Loving Memory of:

My Mother, Marilyn
(August 1943 - February 1983)

My Maternal Grandmother, Ethel
(February 1915 - May 1983)

My Son, Brandon
(July 1992 - March 1993)

My Father, René
(September 1939 - November 2001)

My Paternal Grandmother, Juliette
(September 1918 - October 2003)

DISCLAIMER

This book comes from my history as a granddaughter, daughter, and sister of a family experiencing an inordinate amount of cancer. I am not a professional health care provider but rather an informed individual who cares deeply about my health and the health of my family. **This book does not replace medical care and advice.** Instead, it encourages informed collaboration with health care professionals such as family doctors, cancer specialists, and genetic counselors. With the availability of genetic counseling and predictive testing, it is easier now to identify increased risk factors that may lead to higher rates of breast or ovarian cancer in our families.

My decisions for preventive health care are not necessarily best for other people with similar concerns and family history. Choices must be weighed according to each person's psychological makeup, religious beliefs, marital and family situation, and other factors. **I offer my choices as illustrations rather than guidance.**

I urge you to take responsibility for your own health. Learn all you can about your personal and familial health risk and what you can do to prevent cancer and other diseases. Looking for or even identifying a genetic risk factor does not have to interfere with your plans for a full and rewarding life. It might even save your life and the lives of your children and grandchildren.

I wish you the best of good health.

Although the author has done research to ensure the accuracy of the information contained in this book, she and her associates assume no responsibility for errors, inaccuracies, omissions, or other inconsistency herein. Any perceived slights against people or organizations are unintentional.

Contents

	Dedication	xii
	Foreword	xiii
	Introduction	xv
Chapter 1	The Roots of My Journey	1
	Creating a Genealogy	8
	Taking Action on Your Health	10
Chapter 2	Gifts from My Children	11
	Creating Connections	13
	Taking Action on Your Health	14
Chapter 3	Third Child, Third Gift	15
	Genetic Counseling	17
	Taking Action on Your Health	19
	Research and Internet Support	20
Chapter 4	Gift from My Great Uncle	21
	About Genetics	24
	About BRCA Gene Mutations	25
Chapter 5	My Turn for the Test	27
	Gene Testing	32
	Taking Action on Your Health	34
Chapter 6	Waiting for the Results	37
	My Family	38
	Involving Family Members	39
	Taking Action on Your Health	40

Contents

Chapter 7	The Results of My Genetic Testing	41
	Preventive Options	43
Chapter 8	Getting Doctors on Board	45
	Working with Health Care Professionals	47
Chapter 9	Deciding on Reconstruction	49
	My Decision	52
	Hormone Replacement Therapy	52
	Involving the Children	53
	Taking Action on Your Health	54
Chapter 10	Preparing for Surgery	55
	Concerns of Faith	57
	Taking Action on Your Health	57
Chapter 11	Recovery after Surgery	59
	Post-Surgery Recovery Plans	61
	Post-Surgery Medical Interventions	61
	Womanhood and Sexuality	63
	Taking Action on Your Health	64
Chapter 12	Catching Up: Where I am Now	67

Contents

Appendix A	Am I Next In Line? - Stories	71
Appendix B	Affirmations	99
Appendix C	Making the Decision to be Tested	103
Appendix D	Internet Support	107
Appendix E	Recommended Reading & Resources	113
Appendix F	Glossary	119
Appendix G	Biography	131

DEDICATION

To my husband, Myron, who saw opportunity in gene testing and was with me at every meeting and patiently supported me as I considered so many decisions along the journey to cancer prevention. He encouraged me to find my own answers and vowed to love me no matter what health decisions I made.

To my children, Amanda and Evan, who have compassion and wisdom more profound than many can understand and who share it openly.

To my father, who along with my siblings, grandmother, aunts, uncles, cousins and friends, encouraged me to seek answers to my many questions about cancer risk and prevention. I am grateful for their prayers and support.

To the genetic counselors, doctors and surgeons to whom I entrusted my deepest, most personal fears of dying young. These professionals gave me the courage to investigate and respond to my genetic predisposition towards developing cancer.

FOREWORD

I first met Monique in 1999 when she phoned to introduce herself to the new Director of the Cancer Genetics Research Clinic in Calgary. Monique referred to herself as a "cancer pre-vivor," a term found on the FORCE Web site (www.facingourrisk.org) that stands for survivor of a predisposition to cancer.

Over the years I have worked with many individuals and families as they strive to make sense out of their genetic heritage. A cancer diagnosis has a profound effect on the person receiving the news, as well as their family and friends. When similar types of cancers occur in a family over several generations, this may be an indication of a hereditary cancer syndrome.

In association with the local media and cancer support groups, Monique has worked hard to raise public awareness about hereditary breast and ovarian cancer syndrome. By sharing her experiences, she encourages other families with hereditary cancer syndromes to learn more about their possible health risk, and options for cancer risk reduction.

This book explores the very human side of hereditary cancer syndromes. Monique reflects upon her childhood, filled with love, adventure, joy and companionship. But she was to uncover a dark family secret, the day she innocently walked into her grandmother's room and saw the scars that were the result of her double mastectomies and radiation treatment. Within a few years, Monique was confronted with her own sense of mortality, following her mother's diagnosis of ovarian cancer when Monique was only 16. It was no surprise to hear that Monique assumed she was next in line for cancer.

Monique's journey has opened doors for her family, enhancing communication and creating opportunities for cancer risk assessment and management. This book was written to give hope to families like Monique's, and for the generations to come.

Rhiannon Hughes, MD, MSc, FRCPC, FCCMG
Medical Director, Cancer Genetics Research Clinic, Calgary, Alberta

INTRODUCTION

Each of us is unique because we have a one-of-a-kind genetic makeup. There is nobody else like you or me in the whole world, and we are not like anyone who has ever lived before. Yet we are each linked to the web of family health histories that pre-date and surround us. This is the complexity I have been grappling with since the day my mother was diagnosed with terminal stage III ovarian cancer in 1982, when she was 38 and I was only 16 years of age.

Losing one's mother is profound at any age. My grief was heightened by the realization that a startling number of my immediate and extended family members died young from cancer. The shadow of potential vulnerability to cancer has followed me through my own marriage and motherhood and inspired me to research my family history and genetics and to become an empowered health care user. Surprisingly, I have also come to love the generations of my family more deeply than I otherwise might have, had I not come to recognize and appreciate how profoundly we are connected to one another.

I wrote this book as a way of understanding if I was "next in line" for the cancer that seems to stalk my family. Throughout my journey of genetic discovery, I learned many new words and have included a glossary in **Appendix F** to clarify medical terminology that is used throughout the book.

I hope that by documenting the steps I took to find answers, I can inspire everyone who reads this book to take their own journey towards good health. Please visit my Web site for further information and resource links: **http://www.aminextinline.com**

1

The Roots of My Journey

Family history has always been important to me. My family moved from city to city when I was a child, and although it was exciting to move to a new house and a new school every year, I wanted roots. One way to establish roots for myself was to create a family tree that I could take with me from place to place. It kept me connected to my aunts, uncles, and cousins when we were traveling. It was also another way to ensure I would be in contact with relatives throughout my life, since I was amassing a family treasure – a family genealogy that included stories of travel, immigration, courtship, engagement, and marriage. It also contained health histories.

My concern about a potential genetic cancer gene mutation being found in my family stemmed from the losses of my maternal grandmother and mother. For this reason, I want to share some of the stories collected about my mother's family and encourage you to collect the same kind of stories about your family. They may hold keys to your future health as mine certainly did. I believe that my interest in tracing the family tree and writing down the stories is the reason that the doctors were able to assess my genetic risk for developing cancer and the options available to me.

My maternal grandmother's parents met on a ship coming to America from Europe. When they arrived in New York, they lived in the Jewish community. She was Russian and he was English. They married and had two children. Stories from one generation to the next tell that great grandpa enjoyed reading the works of Charles Dickens while he smoked a pipe and ate chestnuts. My mother also mentioned that distant relatives mourned the loss of several cousins who died of breast cancer. I did not know whether those deceased cousins were from my great grandfather's or great grandmother's side of the family. Much later, I decided to investigate the family history to find out who had died of breast cancer and why my mother had deemed it important enough to mention to me when I was just a girl of twelve or thirteen years of age.

My mother's parents met at a party. After a courtship, they married and had three children: a daughter, who died from lupus erythematosus at age 21; another daughter, my mother, who died of ovarian cancer at age 39; and a son. Grandpa adored his daughters. He recounted a story of how one of his daughters had been shopping and found two coats that she liked and couldn't decide which one to buy. When she called him with her dilemma he told her to buy both on his credit! Grandpa also loved his son very much. They were business partners for many years. My uncle is the sole survivor of my mother's family.

My mother and father met in New York City, and after dating a few years, she became Catholic and they married. Shortly after their wedding, they moved to Canada. This may explain why we did not meet many of the relatives on my mother's side of the family.

When I was a young girl, my grandmother visited us frequently and for a month or two at a time. We loved her very much. Her visits were wonderful because we would have so much fun together. She cooked the most delicious spaghetti sauce, made cheese blintzes, kreplach, apple pie, and matzoh brie. She always brought gifts that she had picked up at the Hadassah Bazaar, where she volunteered. The days were always full as we enjoyed swimming, sunbathing, reading, and playing card games together. These memories are sweet.

A more painful remembrance is of the time I accidentally walked into the guest room where Grandma was changing into her clothes after swimming. I was about nine years old and was very surprised to see that her body was badly scarred. I saw her bra, which looked different from my mother's. It was a prosthetic bra. When she saw my look of surprise, she was taken off guard and asked me to leave the room. Later, my mother and she explained that her scars were the result of a breast cancer treatment from many years before. She had had a bi-lateral mastectomy to save her life. She said that she was glad to be alive, and I agreed, saying that I was happy that she was alive too. I loved her so much. My love for her did not diminish, but never did I want to see her body again. Her body frightened me. I never discussed the matter again with my grandmother.

As I was maturing, my mother taught me to be vigilant about monthly breast self-exams. I didn't think that there was a chance I would develop breast cancer just because my grandmother had. After all, she didn't talk about it as if it was still a concern, and she hadn't died. My mother was in good health and teaching me about breast self-exam was just another lesson like personal hygiene.

My parents shared common dreams, goals, and faith as they traveled North America, living wherever they stopped, and doing business wherever there was a job or a market. I learned to adapt to new situations, homes, schools, curricula, climate, and friends. I was the eldest of six children and we were commanded to be healthy! If any of us dared to say we were sick or not feeling well, my father would announce firmly, "You're not allowed to be sick," and that was that. Throughout my life, my parents insisted that we recognize who our best friends were: our siblings. I learned that although I could be independent in a lot of situations, I could always depend on my family to back me up and support whatever decision I would make, whether academic, professional, or personal.

My childhood was one of adventure and travel. Many experiences gave me the courage and time to think about where I came from and where I wanted to go in my life. I wondered what path I would take in my future, given this uprooted background. When somebody implied that so much traveling made our upbringing "unstable," my father replied that it was not unstable because the family was stable. In retrospect, I know he was absolutely right.

My family celebrated Christmas 1981 in the usual way with lots of love, food, and gifts. Unfortunately, the festivity of the season was marred by a New Year's revelation that my mother's stomach had grown to the size of a watermelon with an undiagnosed tumor. She went to the doctor, and he assured her that it was likely a benign cyst filled with fluid that easily could be drained during a short stay in the hospital.

Just a few days later, on January 12, 1982, my father came home from the hospital and called a family meeting in the kitchen. The so-called benign cyst was actually a malignant tumor. He told us our mother had Stage III ovarian cancer and was terminally ill. She had been given a three to six month prognosis. I left the room heartsick with the news. I tried to imagine what life would be like without my mother, and the thought frightened me. As the eldest of six children, at age sixteen, I thought about how my role as daughter and older sister would change. My youngest sister was only nine at the time. I wondered why this was happening and why the doctors hadn't seen the cancer earlier. Mom had just been to the doctor for a physical check-up in November and was given a clean bill of health, and now, only weeks later, she was dying.

My parents embarked on a life-saving mission, while my brothers, sisters, and I continued to go to school and keep life as normal as possible. Mom tried to do what the conventional doctors recommended but was disgusted with the side effects of chemotherapy and radiation that didn't seem to offer a quality of life or any hope. She swore she'd rather die than mistreat her body like that. She had radiation treatments, changed her diet, and even tried alternative health treatments that were only offered to advanced cancer patients.

That summer, my family took advantage of our summer vacation with a three-week road trip down the west coast of the USA and into Mexico. Although my brothers, sisters, and I considered it one of the best summer holiday trips ever, our parents were actually heading to Mexico to meet yet another doctor offering treatment that might lead to a cure, or at least buy more time.

On other occasions, members of my father's family came to stay with us while my parents searched for alternative treatments in the USA and Mexico. My mother surprised doctors by living six, and finally, nine months longer than they had predicted. She kept a positive attitude about life and lived every moment with newfound appreciation.

Mom celebrated Christmas 1982 with us, and I knew it was probably her last when she quipped, "Jesus made water into wine here on earth, so I'm expecting a party when I get to Heaven!" In February of 1983, my parents were in Houston, Texas chasing one final attempt of treatment when she died in their room as she was going to sleep. It was a one year battle against ovarian cancer. I was 17 years old. My mother was 39.

My mother was not afraid of death. I think she welcomed it after all the ups and downs of her journey living with cancer. She had a strong faith in God. She was a faithful, loving wife, and mother. Then, after so many years of reprieve from breast cancer, my grandmother died two months later at age 68 of colon cancer.

My father, grandfather, and uncle mourned the sudden loss of the women in their lives. We children also mourned, although our family did not address our loss until much later, after everyone else had dealt with the logistics of funeral arrangements, travel, and their own grieving process.

Alone, among my siblings, I felt additional anxiety about the threat of cancer for the rest of my family and me. Besides being told about my grandmother's breast cancer and subsequent colon cancer, and having witnessed my mother's battle with ovarian cancer, I knew that other relatives had died of breast cancer. At 17, it seemed obvious to me, if to no one else, that cancer ran in families, and I was next in line in ours.

This fear of imminent cancer diagnosis stayed with me into my early twenties, when, finally, a 1987 visit with my grandfather in New York offered me a reprieve. Grandpa was genuinely shocked when I casually mentioned my self-imposed prophecy of being next in line for cancer. He quelled my fears by adamantly stating there was no connection between breast, ovarian, and colon cancers and that the breast cancer in our extended family was so distant, it couldn't possibly affect me. His words were a great comfort. I let go of most of my fears. However misguided his opinion turned out to be in light of current medical knowledge, I am still grateful for my grandfather's encouraging words at that time in my life. It was a great loss to me when he suffered a heart attack and died in 1992, a day before the birth of my second child.

The next years of my life were filled with joy and promise. In 1989, I married a wonderful man who shares my interest in good health, entrepreneurial endeavors, faith and family.

Creating a Genealogy

When my interest in following the family tree was kindled, some family members did not want to be involved or share information. So, I focused at first on those family members who were interested – the natural storytellers who loved to recount beloved family tales.

Years later, at a family reunion, I met other relatives displaying the information they had collected on our family tree. By comparing inconsistencies in our information, we were able to create a clearer picture of our family genealogy. From this time on, I was driven to obtain personal accounts to make my reports more accurate. Some members of the family couldn't share any more information than the proper spelling of names, exact dates of birth, and places of origin. However, through further inquiry, I collected employment and statistical information, dates of marriage, and religious affiliation. As the picture became more elaborate and interesting, more members of the family became interested and even said they'd like a copy of my genealogy findings.

While it can be expected that people may feel reticent to share some aspects of their lives and the lives of their ancestors, I was surprised to find health issues on that list. Few people seemed to want health issues on the written record. As I inquired more aggressively about health concerns in the family, even close family members did not want to share such personal information. They claimed to know very little about other members of the family, and if they did, they felt uncomfortable sharing it "third party" for the purposes of genealogy. Discussion of health concerns seemed to be restricted to elicitations of sympathy, prayers, and assistance. Sometimes people simply didn't want to be reminded of the pain and suffering of a loved one and their own feelings of grief and loss.

Despite this apparent taboo, health is one of the most important pieces of the family puzzle to pass on to future generations. It must be written to ensure its accuracy and usefulness. Potential diagnoses can be foreshadowed when this information is shared with a doctor. I tried to convey to my family that when ill health is discussed, it is not necessarily a call for sympathy, but could serve as a warning of a potential risk to others in the family. It is better to be aware of the risk than to pretend that we can't be hurt by what we refuse to recognize.

Well-intentioned friends and family tried to console or dissuade me by making comments such as: "Just because your aunt got it, doesn't mean that you will," or, "Just live your life and God will take you when he wants to," or, "It's a private issue, please don't ask personal questions," or "It's really none of anyone's business."

I am striving to learn how we can encourage the people we love to share this kind of information and trust that our family privacy and our feelings will not be mistreated. It has taken a long time for my family to understand that I don't write our family history for the sake of nosiness or selfish intent, but rather for the benefit of generations to come who will be interested in who we are, what we do, and how we live by staying focused on good health.

Taking Action on Your Health

Draw a family tree or genogram, including names, dates of birth and death, and available health information, including allergies, early childhood illnesses, and other potential genetic anomalies in your family. Go back as far as you can in the family tree and be sure to include all recent members in the family, including newborns and twins. Also note who was right-handed or left-handed. Some of the facts will be important, while others may just be fun or interesting trivia that spell out unique features of your family. This project can be about celebration as well as preventive health care.

Recall times of hardship, challenge, and illnesses that your family has overcome. Think about whom among your parents, siblings, aunts, uncles, and extended family members may be willing to discuss such personal remembrances with you. A questionnaire may be prepared, with the assistance of your counselor, to share with these people, in person, by phone, through mail, or e-mail.

The thought of meeting distant relatives can be exciting and perhaps frightening. Think about how you will be the most comfortable to initiate contact. Be sure to tell them what you will do with the information they share with you.

Take a moment to consider how you feel about sharing health information with relatives you may never have met before. Your comfort level will help others feel comfortable too.

2

Gifts from My Children

When I learned I was pregnant for the first time, I was ecstatic. I was so happy about becoming a mother. My happiness was tempered when I remembered how much my mother had looked forward to sharing the moment with me. When my daughter was born, I recalled how often my mother had repeated the phrases: "When you have children, you'll know" and, "When I'm a grandmother, I'll do this or that..." I felt sad for her loss, even though I was excited about my new baby. I prayed I would be a good mother and be blessed with a long life – long enough to see my grandchildren and great grandchildren grow.

It was another happy day when I discovered I was pregnant with our second child, but that excitement diminished 18 weeks later when an anomaly was seen on a routine ultrasound. The doctors explained that my baby was suffering a blockage in his ureter and this was preventing normal kidney development. This anomaly catapulted my husband and me into a quest for information on kidney failure and renal transplant. At 29 weeks, the doctors strongly recommended amniocentesis to evaluate the viability our son's lung development before the C-section delivery. We agreed to this procedure because we wanted to know if our son could be promised a reasonable quality of life, even, perhaps, as a special needs child. Our son's test confirmed normal chromosomal development and his lungs were strong enough to allow his early arrival at 31 weeks gestational age.

We learned a lot about medical personnel and how they come to make serious decisions with the help of patients and their guardians. We were told that it would be best to either let the doctors attempt an experimental procedure on our newborn, or do nothing and see how he would fare on his own until he was big enough to better handle dialysis. We chose the latter. As we were leaving the nephrologist's office, we held hands and said, "Thank you." After a very short pause, the doctor stated, "By the way, statistically speaking, you two will be divorced in six months."

This was very disheartening for me to hear. My husband, on the other hand, appreciated the doctor's candor, and when times got difficult, we remembered those words and swore that our relationship would survive no matter what. After so much love, care and numerous medical procedures sustained his seven months of life at the hospital, nurses, doctors, volunteers, friends and family joined us at our infant son's funeral.

A few weeks later, we met with the geneticist at the Children's Hospital for a final follow up assessment. We were given a report that indicated there was not likely a genetic link to the challenges our son encountered. In other words, his kidney blockage was a "fluke." We were encouraged to have more children without the fear of another child having renal problems.

I didn't realize at the time that the obstetrician/gynecologist who delivered my son and the medical geneticist who met with us after his death, would become strong advocates for my health only a year or so later. Our son's life holds extra special meaning to us for this reason.

Creating Connections

Overcoming the medical challenges during our son's short life taught us that in extreme situations, some people you expect to be with you through the good and bad times may not be as well prepared to handle it as you need them to be. These dear friends and family never seemed to say the right thing but did their best to show genuine concern. At the risk of losing our relationship, they offered opinions and played "devil's advocate" to encourage us to think of all possibilities of care. For these reasons, I learned to trust doctors and specialists and to respect and nurture my relationship with these professionals. I learned to stop complaining about the health care system and to be grateful that there is a system.

My new understanding of the health care system and those directly involved with it, including doctors, nurses, and support staff helped me later when my own health became a concern and an issue of prayer, discernment, and dialog.

Taking Action on Your Health

List people in the medical profession you have met during the illness of a family member. They may have information that directly pertains to your family health context or medical care.

Do you have friends in the health care field who may be able to give you referral to specialists and insight into the professional reputation of health care providers?

Review the skills you have developed as a care provider and an advocate for your family members during their times of illness. Which of these skills can you bring to bear as you advocate for your own health?

3

Third Child, Third Gift

We were sitting in a doctor's office for our third child's second year check-up. My husband was reading a magazine and noticed an article highlighting some new findings in cancer genetics. A gene mutation had been identified on chromosome 17. The mutation was most often found in people with Ashkenazi (Eastern European) Jewish heritage, among other identified groups with a history of marriage within their own community.

A blood test could identify a carrier of this mutation, alerting the patient to an increased risk of breast or ovarian cancer, now known to be biologically linked. A person's family cancer history might make them a candidate for gene testing. Sitting there in that doctor's office, holding my baby, all of my buried fears resurfaced.

The article detailed many other issues with which we would soon become all too familiar. Genetic testing might cause stress and even collapse of personal relationships with immediate and distant family members. Health and life insurance coverage might be compromised. Employment might be jeopardized. It was too much to take in all at once.

The article further recommended that family doctors refer patients to a genetic counselor or a medical geneticist who would be familiar with the information and available research studies. I decided that rather than asking our family doctor for a referral, I would contact the medical geneticist with whom we already felt comfortable – the person that we met a short time after our first son's death. I made an appointment to see him.

During the first appointment with the medical geneticist, we charted my family tree. We focused on information from my mother's side of the family since it showed a possible hereditary cancer factor with several occurrences already documented. We mapped three or four generations and were careful to include health information coming through the men and women of my mother's side of the family tree because genetic information is passed to the next generation through both parents. Suddenly, my family genealogy interest grew from an entertaining hobby to an important component of my health care plan. The diagram of my family's health history clarified my concerns.[1]

The medical geneticist compared this information to published tables and risk calculation models to determine whether a BRCA gene mutation might be responsible for the cancer in my family. In the end, he determined that testing for a possible BRCA gene mutation was an option for my family and me. He gave a brief overview of family cancer genetics and strategies that could be followed to evaluate my risk. He also recommended a physical examination including a clinical breast exam and a pelvic exam, noting that I would also have a mammogram, a pelvic ultrasound and a CA-125 test to start an early surveillance regimen.

Genetic Counseling

Genetic counseling brings family members together to discuss health issues in a clinical setting with professionals trained to recognize hereditary risk factors and support people as they consider and perhaps, go through gene testing. Genetic counseling can involve a team of professionals, including a genetic counselor and a medical geneticist, and in the case of cancer, an oncologist, surgeon,

[1] Information about health problems that occur more than twice in a family may be factors that indicate a hereditary or genetic concern and should be recorded.

or gynecologist. The process of counseling will likely require a number of visits to fully examine all the issues, with sessions prior to gene testing, between testing and the release of results and post-results. In the United States, health insurance may or may not pay for every session, depending on your plan. However, in Canada, all clinic appointments are covered by provincial health insurance.

Genetic counselors are health professionals with specialized graduate degrees and experience in the areas of medical genetics and counseling. Most enter the field from a variety of disciplines, including biology, genetics, nursing, psychology, public health and social work. Medical geneticists (MDs) complete five years of specialty training in medical genetics after they graduate from medical school. You can locate a genetic counselor by accessing the National Cancer Institute, the National Society of Genetic Counselors and the Canadian Association of Genetic Counselors Web sites (see Appendix E). Your family doctor can give you a referral, or you may be able to set up an appointment yourself. Some genetic counselors are at regular medical genetics clinics that might be located in adult or children's hospitals.

To be accepted as a patient for genetic counseling, you must meet certain criteria. This list of criteria is generic and may be modified by different clinics. In my case I met both of the criteria outlined at the local genetics clinic:

- three or more blood relatives over at least two generations have been diagnosed with similar types of cancer or with different cancers that are part of a known hereditary cancer syndrome such as hereditary breast and ovarian cancer – HBOC

• and ...one relative diagnosed with cancer before the age of 55

Some cancer syndromes can be diagnosed by a doctor, based on physical examination or tests (e.g. colonoscopy). Consult with your local cancer genetic counselor to determine if you are a candidate for genetic counseling.

The genetic counseling we received was a great help to my husband and me. My assessment indicated an increased cancer risk, so the genetic counseling sessions included discussion of cancer risk management strategies and options for gene testing. The counseling helped me explore feelings about my potential risk status and make a healthy adjustment to that risk status. It also brought to light the important issues of confidentiality. I began to feel that I would have a chance to beat the cancer I thought I would be destined to develop.

Even though I initiated the counseling, the information I received and the options that were offered had serious implications for others in my family, especially my sisters and relatives outside the country. Some of my immediate family members accepted my invitation to attend a joint appointment with the genetic counselor, and others did not. I respect the decision of each person.

Taking Action on Your Health

Do you have a family history of cancer that is suggestive of inherited cancer susceptibility? Do you have three or more relatives diagnosed with similar types of cancer or with different cancers that are part of a known hereditary cancer syndrome such as BRCA1 or BRCA2 (breast, ovarian, prostate, or colon cancer)?

Are there any cancer survivors in your family? Have they, or would they, consider genetic counseling?

Would you consider genetic counseling for yourself? Why or why not?

Research and Internet Support

I have found the Internet to be a tremendous tool for accessing information anytime, day or night. However, some of the information on the Internet that appears to be legitimate may in fact be unsound. Collect information you deem to be trustworthy and make sure to share it with your doctor or genetic counselor. They can help you discern and understand what information is relevant to you. I found the process of collecting information to be a very rewarding proactive exercise.

I highly recommend starting at the Web site of the reputable non-profit organization Facing Our Risk of Cancer Empowered (FORCE). You will find it at http://www.facingourrisk.org.

4

Gift from My Great Uncle

While it is possible that my family history and ethnic heritage together could have made me a candidate for gene testing, there was one preferred step to take first: testing a cancer survivor in the family and identifying a potential gene mutation. If a BRCA gene mutation was identified in that person, other members could be contacted and offered genetic counseling plus the possibility of a gene test. This was explained as the preferred course of action - with, of course, the necessary counseling for the consenting survivor.

In my case, this step was not possible, since there were no longer cancer survivors in my immediate family who could be tested. Under the advice of my medical geneticist, I agreed to contact my great uncle (my maternal grandmother's brother) in the United States and request a sample of his blood for gene testing. It was a long shot in the sense that he was never diagnosed with cancer. But the medical geneticist determined that it was worth investigating whether he was carrying a gene mutation, since his sister had been diagnosed with breast cancer and died of colon cancer. Like many of the men in affected families, he might not have developed cancer, but he could certainly be a gene mutation carrier. It should also be noted here that studies show that men who do carry the gene mutation have an increased lifetime risk of male breast cancer, colon cancer and prostate cancer.

My great uncle was 77 years old when I called him in 1994. He had suffered a stroke, and as a result, his short-term memory was poor. His excitement started to build as he recounted the stories of growing up with his sister—my grandmother and his niece—my mother. He put names to faces on old photographs that I had inherited but could not identify. Through photographs, he introduced me to his first wife and the two children they had before she died (of cancer).

He later remarried and had one daughter with his new wife. When he told me of the death of his youngest daughter at age 32 of breast cancer, I mustered the courage to ask him if he would provide blood for the purpose of cancer genetic testing. To my relief, he agreed. I felt the results, whether positive or negative for the gene mutation, would help settle some of my questions about the cancer histories of my mother, grandmother, and now his daughter.

With my great uncle's permission, our medical geneticist agreed to test his blood for the three common Ashkenazi BRCA gene mutations (two on BRCA1 gene and one on the BRCA2 gene). A nurse drew a sample of his blood in November 1994 and sent the vial directly to our local hospital by air courier. I am grateful to my great uncle for agreeing to participate and also for the timing of our efforts, since he died before knowing the results of his test.

These were not easy months for me as I waited for the test results. Fortunately, the genetic counselor and medical geneticist used the time to set out a high-risk surveillance program based on what was already published in the medical literature. This plan included monthly breast self exams, annual clinical breast exams, annual mammograms (which may begin between age 25 and 35, depending on family history, and breast tissue density), CA-125 tumor marker blood tests, and pelvic ultrasounds to examine the ovaries. I agreed to these measures. These surveillance steps helped me feel that I was taking an active role in being vigilant about my health. I also spent a great deal of time doing my own research on cancer prevention.

As a potential carrier of an Ashkenazi BRCA gene mutation, I became more informed about the responsible measures necessary to promote general good health. I learned that the key factors to pay attention to include: following a good diet of low fat choices and moderate sized food servings and minimal alcohol consumption; being active in a variety of mental and physical challenges; managing stress with relaxation techniques; and getting plenty of sleep each night. I have incorporated these strategies into my daily routine.

Finally, in January 1997, the news was finally in: my great uncle's test result was positive for a BRCA1 gene mutation that was common among hereditary breast and ovarian cancer (HBOC) families of Ashkenazi ancestry.

About Genetics

Human characteristics (traits) are inherited on 23 pairs of chromosomes - half from the mother and half from the father. Each chromosome is made of a long strand of DNA. Along each strand of DNA are different genes. Genes are, for the most part, recipes for proteins. The unique genetic message or "expression" that we each have defines such traits as eye color or hair color or whether we have a dimple like Mom's or not. Science has discovered set rules of genetic inheritance that govern the passage and expression of our genes. The Human Genome Project has successfully completed the sequencing of the entire human genome. Work is ongoing to identify all of the individual genes (an estimated 50,000 unique recipes).

Consider the chromosome as the "library" and each gene can be thought of as a "book" in the "library". The "books" have many "words," and a gene mutation can be compared to an error as small as a missing period at the end of a sentence, or a reversal of two letters in a word or the deletion of many chapters. Within the multitude of genes that have been named, some differences have been identified in people who have been diagnosed with certain diseases or disabilities. These disease-linked differences are referred to as gene mutations. We cannot control the existence of a gene mutation in our family any more than we can control whether our family members inherit a certain hair or eye color.

About BRCA Gene Mutations

Everyone has the BRCA genes. They are tumor suppressor genes within the human body. So far, two BRCA genes have been identified, called BRCA1 and BRCA2. They are located on two different chromosomes. Testing has identified hundreds of different mutations in these genes. Most BRCA gene mutations are unique to a particular family, although others can be relatively common with in a particular population or ethnic group. These mutations are responsible for the gene not doing its tumor-suppressing job on breast and ovarian tumors. One of the common BRCA1 gene mutations is called 185delAG, which is a mutation in exon 2 that can be likened to the second of its 24 chapters. The mutation is the deletion of two letters, AG, following the 185th letter in exon 2. There are three common genetic mutations (two in BRCA1 and one in BRCA2) that are sometimes also referred to as Ashkenazi BRCA mutations, since they are most often found in people of Eastern European Jewish heritage, although they also occur in other ethnic groups.

The likelihood of an inherited BRCA gene mutation resulting in a diagnosis of breast cancer in men or women, ovarian cancer in women, or prostate cancer in men is the subject of much scientific research. Work with your doctor, medical geneticist, and genetic counselor to ascertain the current state of knowledge about the level of risk posed by the particular gene mutation under consideration.

5

My Turn for the Test

With this confirmation of genetic risk, the next phase of my journey began in earnest. For me, once I knew I was a candidate, making the decision to be tested was easy. The bigger question, which I wanted to answer before taking the test, concerned the course of action I should choose if the test indicated I carried a gene mutation and when and how I should involve the rest of my family who might also be implicated by the results.

I detail here information I received at the time from the medical geneticist and genetic counselors who worked with me, as well as material I learned through my own research. I offer it as the basis for my own decisions and not necessarily as the basis that should determine the decisions of others. Research continues to change the knowledge available at a given time. I urge anyone in a similar circumstance to base their decisions on the scientific knowledge of their time and not of mine.

In 1997, when I was making my decision about testing and a subsequent course of action, scientific knowledge indicated that inheriting a BRCA gene mutation could elevate my risk for breast and ovarian cancer up to as high as 85 percent and 65 percent respectively. The genetic counselor explained that risks are generally stated as ranges rather than precise figures. The risk for breast and ovarian cancer was actually within the ranges of 56 – 85 percent and 26 – 65 percent respectively, before age 70.[2] However, a more recent study reveals ominous confirmation that women who carry the BRCA gene mutations are, in fact, at high risk for breast cancer (as high as 82 percent to age 80 as compared to 13 percent in the

---

[2] Studies that were not public at the time tended to support the lower end of the range for women who inherit the Ashkenazi BRCA gene mutations. See Struewing et al 1997; and Satagopan et al, 2001.

general population) and that younger women with the gene mutation are more likely to develop (or be diagnosed with) the disease at an earlier age than were previous generations of carriers. The study also found that carriers born after 1940 had a 67 percent risk of developing breast cancer by age 50, compared with the risk of only 24 percent at age 50 among the carriers born before 1940. The reason is unknown. The BRCA gene mutations also greatly increase a woman's risk of ovarian cancer, being responsible for as much as 10 percent of all ovarian cancer. For BRCA1 gene mutation carriers, the risk is 54 percent and for BRCA2 gene mutation carriers, the risk is 23 percent, compared with a risk in the general population of approximately two percent.[3]

I had what might be a unique response to these risk rates. The risk rates were calculated based on a life span of 70 years, but I had a self-imposed life span of only 40 years based on my family history. I spoke with my genetic counselor of this concern, of how I felt that I was at higher risk (with no medical or statistical foundation) because of my family history. I tried to look at the positive side, by rationalizing that this was my opportunity to make a decision to be more proactive about my health in my early thirties. Even so, I knew that a positive result did not mean that I'd get cancer like so many in my family. I knew that it indicated that I had an elevated risk. It was stressed in the counseling session, for example, that in most individuals with a genetic predisposition to cancer, the gene might not be fully penetrant (about 85 percent penetrance). So, even if an individual is a gene carrier, there is a 15 percent chance that they will not develop the familial cancer, based on the statistics at that time.

---

[3] Abstract: King et al., *Breast and Ovarian Cancer Risks Due to Inherited Mutations in BRCA1 and BRCA2*, Science 2003 302: 643-646

It seemed clear to me that a positive result for a BRCA gene mutation would give me a great deal of information about my health risks. But what would a negative result tell me?

It seemed that the surest thing a negative BRCA cancer gene test result would tell me was that I did not have the gene mutation to pass on to my children. That would be wonderful news. It would also mean that I would not be at increased risk for developing ovarian cancer. Instead my risk for developing ovarian cancer would be the same as any woman in the general population - about 1 in 70 women who live to age 85.

I learned that most people with hereditary breast and ovarian cancer syndrome do not have a BRCA1 or BRCA2 gene mutation.[4] There are likely many more BRCA genes lurking that have yet to be discovered and identified. However, in my family, a BRCA1 gene mutation was identified in my maternal relatives, providing opportunities for other relatives to undergo testing for this same mutation.

The genetic counselor and I agreed there are a variety of factors that influence the development of cancer and other diseases, and that I would always have to be vigilant about the usual surveillance and lifestyle choices needed to maintain good health. This helped calm my repeated questions about what I should do with a negative test result.

We also talked many times about the psychological implications of testing and of the different possible results. The genetic counselor

[4] The provincial labs, in Alberta, Canada, for example, only detect BRCA gene mutations in 25 percent of the families that meet the criteria for HBOC. (ref. Dr. Rhiannon Hughes, personal comm.)

cautioned that studies of other hereditary conditions show that some people become distressed or experience a surge of disappointment if a genetic test result comes back negative. Sometimes divisions are created within families, where people who test negative, feel they don't fit in with the rest of the family – with those who tested positive.

I was provided with the following treatment options in the event of a positive result for the BRCA1 gene mutation: participation in a cancer trial where I could be offered a placebo or a cancer drug (Tamoxifen) to determine whether it helped prevent the diagnosis of breast cancer; prophylactic oophorectomy, that is, the removal of the ovaries to reduce the risk of ovarian cancer; and/or prophylactic mastectomy, removal of the breast tissue with or without reconstructive surgery. I was told that each of the surgeries would reduce my risk by about 95 - 97 percent for breast and ovarian cancer. Again, I caution that this was the best scientific knowledge we had at the time and these options applied only if I was a BRCA1 gene mutation carrier.[5]

Whichever option I chose, relevant high-risk surveillance techniques, including mammography, a clinical breast exam, CA-125 tumor marker blood test, pelvic and transvaginal ultrasound would be important annual follow up examinations.

Although a bit unusual, the counselor and medical geneticist also told me that I could get tested and then postpone learning the results until I was ready and had determined the course of action

---

[5] Bilateral prophylactic mastectomy reduces the risk of breast cancer in women with BRCA1/2 mutations by approx. 90 percent. (ref. Rebbeck et al., J Clin Oncol. 2004 Mar 15;22(6):1055-62)

I would take in the event of a positive result. I think this offer also reflected the political climate of the time. There were many alarming media reports coming out of the USA, and to a lesser extent Canada, portraying gene testing as a "Pandora's box" for the client. The reports suggested that insurance companies had reason to expect notification of testing and the results, and that insurance coverage could be denied if it was learned that a BRCA gene mutation had been discovered and not disclosed to the company as a pre-existing condition.

My husband participated in these counseling sessions. He helped me decide about testing and my plans for self care. In the end, I chose to be tested for the BRCA1 gene mutation – to request prophylactic surgery of my ovaries and perhaps my breasts, if the test indicated I had inherited the BRCA1 gene mutation already identified in my family. Whatever the results, I would continue with the already implemented high risk cancer surveillance.

The test itself was a simple procedure for me. My blood was drawn and given to lab technicians, who examined its properties to see whether my DNA contained the BRCA1 gene mutation that had already been identified in my family.

Gene Testing

BRCA gene testing is a very complex task. It is not available for the average person. In my case, the test was available because the BRCA1 gene mutation had been previously identified in a relative – my great uncle.

I saw many benefits of taking the test after the gene mutation had been identified in my family, including the elimination of my uncertainty about my inherited risk, the potential to reduce my risk through various strategies, and the chance to offer similar information and risk reduction options to others in my family.

I also became aware of the risks associated with testing for a cancer gene mutation, including: psychological distress through the two month long testing process and any resultant treatment; financial costs of some preventive treatments; strained or altered relationships within the family; feelings of guilt about possible transmission to my children; and potential insurance, employment, and social discrimination.

Armed with this knowledge, I did what I could to increase the benefits and decrease the risks. For example, I reminded myself that having a BRCA gene mutation does not necessarily mean I would get cancer. It is not a death sentence or something that needs to cause excessive worry. In my opinion, quality of life is in the living.

I went to seminars, watched television news specials, and read magazine articles to gain insight from brave men and women who took a stand for their health. They shared, publicly, their decision to go through with BRCA gene testing and be proactive in their personal health. Their actions were different, depending on their personal lifestyle, beliefs, and whether or not they had children. It was a great comfort for me to know there were options after the test results were received.

In some provinces or states, there may be a policy in place that restricts testing for an unknown family mutation to only people who have been diagnosed with a cancer characteristic of hereditary cancer syndrome. This may mean that if there are no living, affected relatives who are willing to have gene testing, none is available for the family. Myriad Genetic Laboratories is an

American company and one of the leaders in cancer predisposition testing. This lab provides private testing services for a variety of hereditary cancer syndromes. I encourage you to speak to your genetic counselor and medical geneticist about what is available to you and at what cost. If gene testing is too expensive to consider, be encouraged to know that only five percent or fewer diagnoses of cancer are related to BRCA1 or BRCA2 gene mutations. And only 25 percent of hereditary breast or ovarian cancer diagnoses have a BRCA1 or BRCA2 gene mutation. According to my doctor's recommendation for my situation, increased cancer surveillance, in the way of annual clinical breast exams, mammograms, pelvic and transvaginal ultrasound, and possibly CA-125 tests, are part of a well-organized cancer health watch plan.

Taking Action on Your Health

Does someone in your family have breast, ovarian, or colon cancer? Might this person be a carrier of a gene mutation?

Would this person consider having testing done to identify a familial BRCA gene mutation?

How would you approach this person to inquire about their interest in gene testing?

Write down some of your concerns about the possible consequences of gene testing. Are you concerned about family issues? About insurance issues?

If you decide to have testing, with whom will you share your hopes, your fears, and your concerns?

What are your reasons for making the decision to be tested?

If you decide to postpone or decline gene testing, what are your reasons? And when, if ever, would you choose to reconsider your decision?

How would you react to an affirmative answer? A negative answer?

Is gene testing an option that is available in your town or city?

If not, what are other ways of assessing your cancer risk?

What can you do right now to reduce your risk of a potential cancer diagnosis?

6

Waiting for the Results

Despite the decisions I had made, so many questions went through my mind during the difficult weeks of waiting for my test results. What if it's positive? What if it's negative? What will I really do when I know the results? Will I go through with prophylactic surgery as planned, or will I change my mind at the last minute? How will my husband support me when I don't know what I want to do? How will I explain this concern to others in my family? To be a responsible family member, how many relatives do I have to tell and at what risk to our relationship? What if my sisters test differently than I do?

My plan included a session with the genetic counselor after I took the test and before the results were known. Some experts suggest that this is the time to make plans in the event of a positive test result, including plans for notifying, educating, and counseling other relatives. In my case, some of my family members had chosen to attend a joint session.

My husband was a great support. Together, we decided that our children were too young to be involved, and since I was not ill, they had no reason to be notified. I think my husband and I did a good job of shielding them from our discussions and feelings of uncertainty and fear.

My Family

This is a book about my personal story and I share only my experiences. I respect others in my family for their choices. I respect their privacy. Each of my family members thought deeply on the matter in their own way. We spoke to our God, our friends, family, doctors, therapists, counselors, and even supportive individuals on the Internet about the potential risks and benefits of gene testing and how to deal with the results. As a family, we agreed that our respective decisions were the best ones for us at the time, based on the information we had and our individual circumstances. We were not better or worse, smarter, or dumber for our choices. We were entitled to our own personal preference and comfort level with any particular aspect of a life decision.

My family has provided me with a great deal of emotional support, and we remain close.

Out of curiosity and concern for others in my extended family, I called one of my grandmother's cousins to inquire about which great grandparent might have carried this gene mutation. I learned that it was most likely my great grandfather's side. I felt an obligation to let the potentially affected, although distant, family members know about this information. I didn't receive a reply.

Over the past few years I have developed friendships with both women and men, who struggle with their potential health risk due to a family history of breast or ovarian cancer. We call each other "coping companions." They have also provided me with a great deal of love and support. [See their stories included in Appendix A of this book.]

Involving Family Members

When a person considers a life decision, it is only natural to approach friends and family for support. As much as I appreciated and respected their good intentions to encourage me to reflect on many important issues, at times, the concerns they raised led me to feel conflicted. A few strongly suggested that I avoid surgery or chemical cancer trials, and instead, focus on a more conservative lifestyle and diet. This recommendation, although somewhat harmless, did not come from the doctor or specialists. Friends and natural health practitioners, who usually had herbal supplements to sell, offered their products as cancer preventive measures. Others suggested that I follow an alternative diet, including naturopathic herbs and natural foods with high anti-oxidants and concentrated substances such as Aloe vera juice. Some even challenged me to consider consequences that my decision(s) might have on my soul, with warnings that I might be infringing on God's ultimate plan for my life.

The bottom line is that my family and friends had good intentions and hoped that my decisions would not lead to personal regrets later.

I chose to stay focused on the medical professionals as they exuded confidence and optimism supporting my decisions.

Taking Action on Your Health

How might your decision to have gene testing affect your relationship with your parents, siblings, and extended family?

Might your friendships become stronger as you demonstrate courage and interest in new health information?

7

The Results of My Genetic Testing

I was grateful that my husband agreed to be with me when I received my test results. He had been with me through the counseling sessions and was included in the dialog that led to my plans for self care. Had I been single, I am sure it would have been important for me to have a sibling or close friend by my side to help me receive and accept the information.

Test results are rarely given over the telephone. The genetic counselor and the medical geneticist invited me to their office at my earliest convenience. On the way to the cancer genetics clinic, I was preoccupied with a thought that the results would likely be positive. I was getting worked up over the possibility of hearing that I carry the mutation responsible for cancer that had taken the lives of my grandmother, my mother, and a cousin. I hoped with all my might that I was getting stressed out for no reason, since it was possible I would hear my results were negative. My husband, on the other hand, had a different thought in his mind. He was hoping that my sisters would choose to have testing and that our close relationship would not be affected by our test results if they turned out to be different.

The medical geneticist and the genetic counselor wasted little time with preliminaries and quickly gave me the results of my test. I had tested positive for the BRCA1 gene mutation (185delAG) previously detected in my great uncle.

My knee-jerk reaction was that this news was as devastating as it might have been if I'd been told that I had cancer. What got me through the waves of fear and anxiety was a strong sense of "I know what I have to do now."

I decided to stick with my plan and have a prophylactic mastectomy and oophorectomy. My reasons? I wanted to reduce my risk as much as possible, as soon as possible.

The genetic counselor and my doctor supported my decision. I was given a referral to a gynecologist/oncologist to discuss prophylactic hysterectomy and oophorectomy. I was also given a referral to a breast cancer surgeon to discuss prophylactic mastectomies.

Preventive Options

The medical options available to people who have been identified as carrying a BRCA gene mutation depend on various factors. These factors include where you live, your insurance coverage, family, friends and clergy support, your views about alternative health care (visualization, natural diet remedies, exercise regimes, music for healing, etc.) and preventive surgery. I live in Canada, where the health care system covered the cost for the testing and subsequent treatment, including surgery.

I would encourage anyone on this journey to work with a health care team to assess current medical knowledge – to appreciate how likely each option is to reduce your cancer risk and how the options work together.

8

Getting Doctors on Board

I soon learned that arranging for surgery wasn't going to be as easy as the referral process made it sound. The first two breast surgeons I approached refused to remove perfect, healthy breasts from a 31 year-old wife and mother. They did not deem this surgery as medically necessary.

With the help of my genetic counselor, I was able to get an appointment with an oncologist to discuss a preventive oophorectomy. The visit to the oncologist also showed me that I didn't quite fit in at the Cancer Center. When I called to confirm my appointment, the receptionist wanted to know what my cancer diagnosis was. When I explained I didn't have cancer and was trying to prevent it, she said their oncologists only saw cancer patients. I would have to go elsewhere. I told her the oncologist had agreed to see me, even though I did not have cancer. Since the phone call to the receptionist had been a little hostile, when I arrived for my appointment, I felt self-conscious. I knew that everyone in the room except me had been diagnosed with cancer. I felt like an intruder. Some volunteers came by with a cart of tea and cookies served on fine china. I felt this treat was not meant for me. It was a service offered by a benevolent group for cancer patients, and I wasn't one. They insisted I partake, so I did.

I asked my genetic counselor for information to give to doctors so they would understand why this surgery was medically justifiable. During the meeting with the oncologist, she performed a short examination and agreed that preventive surgery might be a good option. She said, however, she would not perform the surgery on a healthy patient. She suggested I choose a gynecologist not associated with the Cancer Center and then referred me, coincidentally, to the gynecologist who had delivered my daughter and my first son.

After a few months of information gathering and sharing, several medical professionals began to see the validity of the cancer genetic testing and the benefit of all the options available to people, like me, who are at high risk and want to avoid a cancer diagnosis through the prophylactic surgery. In the end, I found skilled and supportive surgeons who agreed to perform my surgery.

Working with Health Care Professionals

Often patients believe that they can only see their doctor when they're sick, but doctors are available to help you stay well. It may be a good idea to let the receptionist know that you wish to make the appointment with your doctor for discussion only. Arrive on time for the appointment and be prepared to spend only a few minutes with the doctor. Leave a letter or some notes for the doctor to peruse a little later. Sometimes people are afraid to ask questions. They fear they may sound silly. In reality, your doctor would like to hear any question on your mind and will welcome new information. Any qualified doctor will agree you have a better chance of good health when you understand the what, why, and how of it. If you do not understand your doctor's explanation, keep questioning until you are satisfied that you do understand. Your physician will appreciate it. Keep a blank sheet of paper in a convenient place, and every time a question comes to mind, write it down. This way, you will not fail to ask something that has been bothering you. You will have a better chance of beating cancer if you allow your doctor to know your family history and your concerns for being next in line.

For those who live in rural areas and cannot see their specialists regularly, I recommend you keep a journal and make note of any concerns. It is important to get to know your doctors and feel confident in communicating with them. They are trained to be sympathetic and understanding about your concerns, especially when your friends, family, and clergy may not be.

9

Deciding on Reconstruction

To help with my deliberations on the option of preventive mastectomy, I called the Canadian Cancer Society and asked to meet a cancer survivor who had chosen a preventive mastectomy without reconstructive surgery. The receptionist directed me to the Society's breast cancer survivor group called Reach for Recovery. I called the contact name and was invited to meet Liz at her home. We sat outside on the patio and sipped tea while she told me of losing her mother to breast cancer when she was only eight years old. She lost her grandmother to breast cancer prior to that. Those losses instilled great fear in her. Every day, she would notice the lumpiness of her breasts and would fret that a breast cancer diagnosis was around the corner. Time after time, the doctors assured her that many girls and women have benign lumpiness and she needn't worry so much.

Liz, however, could not let go of the worry and decided that psychologically, if not physically, she needed to relieve herself of the debilitating fear of breast cancer. She saw a breast cancer surgeon and he agreed that in her case, it would be best to remove the breasts. Genetic counseling and testing were not options at that time. She has never looked back. We went into her house, and she offered to show me her chest. I was impressed with how beautiful her skin was. Her chest was as flat as a nine year-old girl's and the scars were very tiny, just at the place where each nipple would have been.

Before leaving, Liz encouraged me to attend a Reach for Recovery group meeting. She said I would meet a few cancer survivors who would be pleased to share their experiences of breast cancer, mastectomy, and reconstructive surgery. I went home and announced to my husband that if a preventive mastectomy would reduce my risk factor as much as I believed it would, living with a flat chest like my new friend's would be worth it. But I also agreed to go to the Reach for Recovery meeting before making a final decision about reconstructive surgery.

Together, my husband and I went to the Reach for Recovery meeting and met two ladies who had been diagnosed with breast cancer. Each had undergone a mastectomy. One had chosen breast reconstruction. The other had not. The woman who had reconstructive surgery was very pleased with her results. Her surgeon was the same one I was scheduled to see. She took me to a corner of the room and asked if I would like a "show and tell." I agreed. She showed me her results and the practically seamless scars. When my husband and I left the meeting, I announced, "That's what I want!"

My husband and I met with a plastic surgeon willing to read the information I had amassed through research on the Internet. He agreed I would be a candidate for plastic surgery and explained the available options.

Given my body proportions, it seemed the Free Flap TRAM procedure was most suitable for me. This surgical procedure uses tissue from the abdomen to reconstruct breasts. It was one of the best procedures of its time. I was amused to discover it was a good thing I had never lost the "baby pouch" that had bothered me for years, since it meant I had enough tissue to maintain my original breast size. To be honest though, size was not my first priority; health was. Some might question how reconstructive surgery pertains to health, but of course it does! Reconstructive surgery, when successful, is very helpful to the heart and soul of a woman – at least to this woman. I was glad to learn there was a type of surgery that could help me keep an important part of my self-image as a woman. It was an appropriate kind of surgery for me.

It was also important to me to make this decision in partnership with my husband. I wanted to ensure that our strong mutual sexual attraction would not be jeopardized by surgery to alter parts of my body that are so integral and important to lovemaking. By "owning" this decision together, we maintained our loving, committed marital relationship.

My Decision

My original plan was for the oophorectomy to be the first order of business, since early ovarian cancer detection is virtually impossible. I felt confident I could stave off the mastectomy by doing breast self-exams and perhaps "catch it early" if breast cancer developed. My gynecologist evaluated all the information I had researched and suggested I have the oophorectomies and mastectomies performed at the same time. At my age of 32, I would have to take hormone replacement therapy to make up for the hormone imbalance that would result from losing my ovaries. At that time, hormone replacement therapy was commonly being used to treat symptoms associated with going through menopause, and to reduce the risk for heart disease and osteoporosis. Subsequent research studies on hormone replacement therapy are still disputed.

Hormone Replacement Therapy

Would you consider taking hormone replacement therapy if you had an oophorectomy?

What are some of your concerns pertaining to hormone replacement therapy?

Involving the Children

In considering how much information we should share with our daughter, then age six and our son, age three, we learned they were primarily concerned with my physical comfort and how long I would be in the hospital. We assured them I wouldn't be in pain, and I would be coming home happy and healthy.

When the opportunity presents itself, we choose to share information with our children in a relaxed manner and according to their developmental stage. Our daughter was ten years old when we visited a science center exhibit. Of the many displays, one explained genetics in simple terms. At this age, she was able to understand a little more about how our bodies work. This gave us an opportunity to discuss the role genes play in our lives. She asked if she was at risk for cancer. I told her honestly, everyone is at risk for cancer. As we progressed through the exhibit, we learned strategies for a healthy lifestyle, including proper diet, good sleep, good hygiene, and benefits of being a non-smoker.

Because there is a 50 percent chance my children have inherited the gene mutation I carry, sometimes people ask me when I would consider having them tested. Since this gene mutation would not likely affect them until they are adults, I have been advised it is best not to raise the issue or create fear before they can make the choice for themselves – whether to pursue genetic counseling and testing.

Based on clinical experience, there are very few children or teenagers who are mature enough to understand the uncertainties associated with inheriting a cancer gene mutation. Most people (and especially children) make up their mind about their personal risk almost immediately after they learn about the condition. This personal evaluation is based on the circumstances under which they receive the information including how worried or affected their parents (or other relatives) were.[6] I hope that medical science will find a way to reduce cancer risk through gene or hormone therapy before my children reach adulthood.

Taking Action on Your Health

What are some of the advantages and disadvantages of sharing this information with the next generation?

Would your doctor help you to make a plan for informing the children?

How will you support your children through the hard times of your journey, including times in hospital and in recovery?

How will you incorporate teachable moments about genetics and healthy living choices?

At what age will you approach your children about their genetic risk? How will you raise the issue and what information will you share?

---

[6] Reference: Dr. Rhiannon Hughes, pediatrician, who has counseled more than 1000 families.

10

Preparing for Surgery

Although to everyone, I appeared very brave, I did have several moments of doubt, fear, and even panic about some of the irreversible decisions I was making. Every time I went to visit the plastic surgeon with a question or a concern, he put it to rest quickly. Any time a friend or a family member would get concerned and throw in a reason why I shouldn't do what I was planning to do, my professional friends quickly put me at ease and calmed my fears.

Fortunately, my surgeons and the hospital were in close proximity to where I lived. Whenever I felt nervous or upset, an appointment was set up to help me become more comfortable with the idea of being very proactive regarding my future health. The doctors explained the procedures in as much detail as I needed.

My most acute panic attack was on the first day of what would be my last menstrual cycle, which also coincided with my late mother's birthday. It was also the day my husband accidentally deleted all of my e-mail files, including a lot of family support and a whole mailbox of letters from the breast cancer group on the Internet that were vital to me at the time. As the number of days to surgery became fewer and fewer, I felt like an elephant was behind me—thump, thump, thump—and my heart would race a little. One of my concerns was the slight risk of not waking up from the anesthetic. I was also worried that, although I would be completely under anesthetic, I might feel the pain of surgery. My worries, like most worries, were unfounded and a waste of time and energy. I survived it all.

I brought a few things to the hospital to comfort me when I woke up from surgery. These personal items included family photographs, music compact discs, lingerie that opens from the front, and my very own pillow.

I also continued to draw strength from my faith. I believe the fact I had an opportunity to make a decision is, in itself, a gift from God. I had a responsibility to make the right decision through prayerful consideration. I believe I have made the decisions right for me.

Concerns of Faith

Faith can be a great source of comfort and strength for anyone involved in preventive health care measures. In my case, faith also brought pain because I was challenged occasionally by members of my faith community to halt my plans and simply accept God's will. However, I believe God had a hand in my journey, by leading me to the specialists that I needed to meet in order to achieve my risk reduction goal. My decisions were made with my heart and mind, and with information gleaned from meetings with professional genetic counselors and thought-provoking discussions with my closest family and friends. I prayed a lot too!

Taking Action on Your Health

Do you have concerns about spirituality or religious teachings that should be discussed with a spiritual advisor or clergy?

Would your spiritual beliefs be compromised by taking part in new technology such as gene testing and recommendations for preventive measures?

11

Recovery after Surgery

After the 16-hour procedure of mastectomy, breast reconstruction, and total hysterectomy, my recovery time in the hospital was 10 days. During that time, I felt that I had conquered the fears that had plagued me since the time of my mother's death.

The breast cancer survivors who had similar surgery warned me that the first day is the worst day for pain and discomfort. They were right and therefore I was not surprised by how uncomfortable I was during the first day after surgery. I was not allowed to eat or drink, but pain relief was available, and I did not hesitate to use it. The four drains attached to me to remove excess fluid were more of a nuisance than painful. Each day after the first was progressively better than the previous. By the third day, I was feeling much, much better. I think the healing process was more tolerable because I was not ill.

When my doctors sent me home to recuperate from the surgery, they instructed me to rest and not lift anything heavier than five pounds for the first few weeks. It was about three or four weeks before I could lift a pot to the stove to cook. A month and a half passed before I could raise my arm comfortably to get dishes from the cupboard. Fortunately, my brother agreed to live with us and help with all the household responsibilities, while my husband worked and I recovered from surgery. My three year-old son wanted me to hold him. Thankfully, a nursing pillow protected sensitive areas so he could sit on my lap.

I found it difficult to walk up and down stairs due to an incision across my abdomen from the free-flap TRAM breast reconstruction. I lived in a two-story home and for the first two weeks, I slept in a recliner chair on the main floor. My brother-in-law gave me a cordless telephone with a headset, which allowed me to work from home and be in contact with my friends. Within three months, I was able to get back to work and to life at home, even though the doctor stressed words of caution not to overextend myself physically and to ensure that I give the inside of my body a year or two to heal fully.

Post-Surgery Recovery Plans

Do you have a plan for your recovery after surgery?

If you have children, do you have a plan for child care during your recovery?

Do you have access to support to help with household management, including light cleaning and cooking?

If sleeping in your bed presents a challenge, do you have alternative sleeping quarters if necessary?

Do you have to go back to work? If not, will there be a financial strain on the family? How will you deal with this challenge?

Post-Surgery Medical Interventions

Post-surgery appointments were set up for me to go back to the plastic surgeon's office for follow up consultations. I had a very mystifying case of blisters that developed on my breasts. After many tests, I was assured that, although this was not normal, it was not a failure in the breast reconstruction. It had to do with how the skin reacted to the surgery. As it adapted to the surgical alterations, the problem soon passed.

The plastic surgeon used skin from an area on my abdomen to patch where the original nipples had been. About six months later, after healing, I was scheduled for day surgery at the hospital for nipple reconstruction. This was a minor surgical procedure done under local anesthetic in just a couple of hours. The doctor explained that the new constructed nipples start out larger in size and the skin naturally shrinks as it heals. About two months later, we made a selection from skin color swatches, choosing a couple that were a few shades darker than my natural skin tone. These were used to tattoo a mottled effect, thereby creating a natural look for the nipples and areola. I have never received a negative comment about the finished look. When I volunteer a "show and tell" to women considering similar surgery, they are always amazed at the result. I don't know what they expect to see, perhaps more scarring or dimpling, but the fact is that when I am topless, I look pretty darned good from all angles!

Within months, I could see the scars were fading. I credit the Aloe vera product I regularly massaged into the scar lines, but the plastic surgeon said that, in his opinion, the massaging action was helping more than the product.

I also began my course of hormone replacement therapy – a regimen my doctors recommended to compensate for the loss of my ovaries. They prescribed a low dose of estrogen, close to what my body would normally produce to maintain natural lubrication and bone strength. The regimen also minimizes the menopausal symptoms, such as emotional anxiety, hot flashes and body sweats that would have followed the surgery. My situation is reviewed with my doctor every six months to ensure the dosage of estrogen is still correct.

Womanhood and Sexuality

After the incisions healed, I felt that my breasts were nice to look at, but they didn't look normal until the nipple reconstruction was done several months after healing was complete. I wrote in a journal, shortly after my nipple reconstruction surgery: "Last week, I got nipples! And already—it's a funny thing, psychologically—I feel really that much more normal!"

My breast reconstruction is so good that I am very comfortable at the swimming pool or the health club dressing room. I can change in front of anyone and nobody gives me a second look. (And I like it that way, thank you!) I can wear any neckline or a dress with a low cut in the front or back. I can wear a bikini and not feel too awkward. I didn't even wear a bikini before my surgery!

Some women though, have told me that their breast reconstruction experience was not as favorable as mine. A few women described their breast reconstruction like, "two hard mounds slapped onto the body to make fake breasts." And given the chance to do it over again, they would choose not to have the reconstruction. Others find it hard to exercise because the implant and the muscles don't look or act like they should, due to scarring or shifting with body movement. Many are very dismayed at the absence of nipple sensation after surgery. Still others who have had the TRAM surgery have expressed regret for their decision for breast reconstruction because of difficulties with abdominal strength and sometimes abdominal discomfort. Your good or bad experience of breast reconstruction may have more to do with the procedure, rather than the type of reconstruction. It is recommended that you discuss the advantages and disadvantages of the different procedures with your surgeon.

My experience is a best-case scenario. All sensation is not lost, although to be honest, sexual pleasure is not the same as before surgery. For me, the changes in sexual appetite and function could be compared to changes that stem from stress and day-to-day life situations. Prophylactic surgical removal of the breasts and ovaries is scary for a woman because it seeks, in physical terms at least, to remove much of what makes her a woman. But she still retains her heart, her soul, and her mind.

My experience has confirmed for me that sexual pleasure comes more from the brain than from any other part of the body. When my husband is touching me, my mind tells me his caress is every bit as wonderful as it was before. With the free-flap TRAM reconstruction, my husband is as pleased with the natural look and feel of my breasts as I am. This experience has enriched us as a couple to move forward in our quest for good health and our decision to love each other unconditionally.

Like any other woman, I worried that our intimacy and my sense of being a woman could be damaged by the surgeries. I wanted to maintain a sense of my sexuality and beauty, so I arranged to have a professional portrait sitting, before and after surgery. I kept those photographs as testaments of my beauty and courage. Now this book replaces those photos.

Taking Action on Your Health

Imagine your roles are reversed, and your partner is facing these cancer risks and has shared this information with you. What would you say? How would you react? This will give you some insight into how your partner may be feeling.

You may find it easier to write your partner a letter than to speak in person, at least in the beginning. If so, take a few moments to write notes about what you would like to say.

Would you consider inviting him/her to see a genetic counselor with you? How could the genetic counselor help you raise issues concerning sexuality?

How will your sexuality be affected by changes to your body? How can you strengthen your sexual self-image? How can you involve your partner?

12

Catching Up: Where I am Now

Now at age 38, as I approach my 39th birthday, I embrace each day with the realization that if I were following my mother's fate, I would be faced with less than one year of life with my family, friends and this world. Cancer claimed the lives of my parents relatively early. I don't want my husband or my children to experience the pain of losing their wife and mother. As one with a high risk of familial cancer, increases in health awareness and improvements in cancer research have led me to a place where I feel confident I can take care of my health responsibly. I see my doctor regularly for check ups. I will agree to have a colonoscopy every three to five years as part of my colon cancer surveillance after I reach 40 years of age.

I know that what I've been through does not guarantee a cancer-free future, but it does give me peace of mind to know that I found vital health information through my family tree and have used it to further reduce my risk of hereditary breast and ovarian cancer.

Coping with cancer risk is not a matter of thinking positively, or of wishing it away and saying, "Hey, Doc, cure me." It is a matter of knowledge. Moreover, it is a matter of becoming educated about every detail of your medical history and using all available resources to empower yourself to good health. I will encourage my children and friends to use every drop of energy to be proactive about their health. Know that you have options. Create a plan of increased early cancer surveillance and don't discount the potential benefits of prophylactic surgery if this is an option your medical professional suggests.

I know that my decisions were the best ones for me at the time, based on the information I found. Decisions to tell, not to tell, to be tested, not to be tested, to insist on more close screening or not, and to go so far as prophylactic surgery or not, were all considerations I grappled with. I spoke to friends and family, doctors, therapists, counselors, and even found peer support on the Internet offering valuable information about the potential risks and benefits, weighing the advantages and disadvantages of every decision that had to be made along the way.

I came up with an analogy. Look how many car manufacturers there are. Think of why a person buys one make of car over another – they weigh their personal or professional needs, and then they look at the added features of each vehicle to select the one that will get them to where they want to go. This is how we make decisions in life. It's no different when considering gene testing. It will be right for some people but not for all. The options will strike each individual differently as to being a real benefit or not. It's important to recognize our differences as people.

When asked if I have any regrets about the process of genetic counseling, testing, and surgery, what comes to mind is something that happened when I was in the hospital recuperating after surgery. A friend came to visit and gave me a mug with the inscription: "No Retreat, No Reserve, No Regrets." This quotation was attributed to Bill Bordon, a missionary to China. That sums up my journey towards good health!

APPENDIX

A

Am I Next In Line? – Stories

Over the past few years, I have developed friendships with several cancer survivors and their families who struggle with a potential health risk due to a family history of breast or ovarian cancer. The quest for maintaining good health is not uncommon, but for some more than others, this search seems more important and more pressing because we are seeing breast and ovarian cancer diagnoses given to women who are younger than 40 years of age. Sometimes poor health can't be foreseen, but families are starting to notice patterns, and this is where genetics becomes an important tool in helping us prevent potential premature disease and illness.

The stories that follow portray issues and concerns that have crossed my mind or have been introduced to me by several men and women I have come to know over the years. I am grateful to Liz, Danielle Hall, Nancy Prouser, and Suzanne Cooper, for writing and allowing their personal stories to be shared here. The other stories, based on true stories, have been shared by a few who wish to remain anonymous. I am grateful for their contribution and have written their stories as if they were authored by them (with aliases).

We hold in common the fear of unknown genetic factors mixed with what is known—family loss—making life very uncomfortable. Many share the daily challenge of waking up in the morning, wondering, "Is this the day when I'll find a lump just like my mother, sister, aunt, or grandmother did?" or "Do I want to get married and have children, knowing that I might pass on a hereditary gene mutation?" or "I don't want to risk premature death, leaving young children without a mother." Each story carries its own profound message of loss, fear, proactive investigation and hope for the future based on new developments in the medical field of cancer genetics. Appendices B and C will assist you in thinking about your own story.

Liz's Story

My mother, grandmother and great grandmother were all diagnosed with breast cancer in their forties. My mother died of it when I was eight. So I grew up fearing that this would be my fate as well. I had my first mammogram in my twenties, to get a baseline reading. For quite a while I was apprehensive about becoming a parent myself because I didn't want to leave a child the way I had been left. And sure enough, when my son was only one year old, my doctor found a large lump in my breast, but luckily it was not cancerous. My breasts were lumpy. Then, every year after that, there was a scare as either the doctor or I would find a lump. Because my breasts were fibrocystic, they were heavy and uncomfortable and there were little jabs of pain all the time. It was an issue I couldn't get away from. I was becoming more fearful and depressed. Eventually I began to feel I was losing control. I didn't know what to do and felt there was nothing I could do.

Then a new doctor referred me to the local cancer center where a surgeon told me about preventive mastectomies. I started to think that this could be the lifeline I was looking for – I felt like I was being swept down a river and this was one branch being extended to me. Yes, it's drastic, but I thought, "I'd give a lot to be able to get rid of this issue and have a worry-free chest" – it seemed to me like a dream come true. There's never a guarantee that you won't get breast cancer, but obviously if you don't have breasts, your chances of getting breast cancer are much less.

It was a hard decision to make emotionally, and I wrestled with it for about four months. Around the same time, a relative by marriage who was about the same age as me, 36, was dying of breast cancer. That prompted me to set a date for surgery. I felt like this huge rock had been taken off my head. It gave me a whole new lease on life.

I didn't have the reconstruction – that decision caused me a lot of distress at the time. But I didn't want to go through with another surgery, especially since they didn't seem to have all the problems worked out with implants. The last thing I wanted was to change one set of chest problems for another. Now I feel 100 percent comfortable with the way I am. My husband has been totally supportive. He wanted me to do whatever would keep me alive and healthy. The bottom line is my life is much better now than it was before.

David's Story

My mother died of ovarian cancer when I was 12 years old. My grandmother died of breast cancer a few months later. At the time, I didn't really give much thought to their deaths as having anything to do with me. Why would I? I'm a guy, and those are "women's diseases," right? Well, I thought so until my sister investigated some genetic studies that showed an increased risk for prostate cancer in males who come from families with a gene mutation that also advances the risk of breast, ovarian, and even colon cancer.

My sister found out the mutation was in our family makeup and asked me to consider genetic counseling for my own information. What could it hurt? Our health insurance agreed to pay for the counseling and the testing if I chose to do it.

I wasn't married at the time, so the results were not going to be a big deal to me, or at least so I thought. I was, however, made aware that if I did test positive for the family mutation, I would be at increased risk for prostate cancer and there was a 50 percent chance that my "future children" would inherit the mutation as well. Again, this was all very hypothetical at the time.

I agreed to the testing, and although it didn't mean a lot to me then, I tested negative. I was told that this was good news and that I am at the average risk for prostate cancer later in life. My children are not at risk at all of receiving the family mutation from me because I don't have it to pass on. It doesn't skip generations, so my grand-children won't be at risk either.

Now I am 30 years old and getting married. We plan on having children, so it is nice to know I am in the clear, as far as this genetic information is concerned. I am also glad that my sister feels that it is so important to share this with family members because not everyone wants to talk about it, or even consider it. I don't have to worry about speaking to my future daughters, or sons about this health worry that could have been a concern.

Janice's Story

My mother died of ovarian cancer two days before my 15th birthday. I felt very sad, but I didn't really think I had anything to worry about, as far as my own health.

Several women in my family had breast, ovarian, or colon cancer and my paternal grandfather died of pancreatic cancer. I thought that maybe I would get cancer sometime in my life, but didn't really think it was something that I had necessarily inherited from my family. Of course, cancer is not contagious.

When I was growing up, I learned that a healthy lifestyle includes eating nutritious foods outlined in the National Food Guide and taking part in regular exercise ensures good health. I also keep an open mind to alternative health therapies that might include taking natural herbs or vitamins to supplement my diet.

One day, my sister called and told me about gene testing that is available for families with a family history of cancer. We went to see the genetic counselor and medical geneticist who were working together. We were informed that a BRCA gene mutation had been identified in our family. I was not married at the time, but planned on getting married in the future and having children. In the spirit of solidarity, I agreed to have the test done at the same time as my sister.

Since my sister was already married and had children, she was pretty sure of how she would respond to a positive test result. I was not really sure what to think for myself. I know that I wanted to hear that the result was negative.

We went to the counselor's office and received our results — we both tested positive. But we had very different ideas on what to do with this information. My sister wanted to have surgery done as soon as possible to reduce her risk for ovarian cancer. I, on the other hand, did not want to have surgery and chose instead, to have increased screening and to start taking birth control pills to reduce the ovulation cycle, which is said to help stave off ovarian cancer.

To this day, I am not sure if it was a good idea that I got tested, because I don't want to risk my health worrying about it.

Since my cancer risk is high, my breast doctor and gynecologist will give keep me on the recommended high surveillance plan of semi-annual mammograms, pelvic and transvaginal ultrasounds, and an annual CA-125 blood test.

I do not know if I will ever agree to preventive surgery. But I will definitely do everything I can to ensure that if there is anything to catch, it will be caught in the early stages and be treated immediately so that I can be a long term survivor.

I hope I will be part of the population that carries the gene mutation but will never hear a cancer diagnosis. After all, 15 - 50 percent of women carrying the BRCA gene mutation never develop breast cancer.

Now I am married and would like to have children. Although it is a fact that the gene mutation can be carried to another generation, I am not going to let that possibility (50 percent) discourage us from having a family.

I hope that advanced gene therapy or repair will be available for future generations to be proactive about their cancer risk.

When people ask me if I am glad that I did the gene testing, I can only answer with, "Sometimes I am, and sometimes I am not." I don't like to talk about it. I especially don't like to discuss it with my family. It's really personal. I don't know if this is the best way to deal with it, but my husband and I want to have children, and so, nothing will stand in our way.

Rachel's Story

My cousin's daughter called me one day, asking about information on our family. I told her that my sister just died of breast cancer. She was in her early thirties. My mother had also died of cancer at a young age.

I was surprised to find that a breast cancer gene mutation is in our family. But it does explain why so many were dying of cancer. My father went for testing, and he is a carrier of the mutation. It was devastating news. We live in the United States and because there is so much controversy and debate over the issues that can affect your whole life, I decided against testing. I did not want to jeopardize my health insurance, my employment, or my family relationships. I especially did not want to find out I might carry a gene mutation that could have been passed on to my children and be leading them to the same fate as my sister.

My daughter thinks she might want to know, but she hasn't had testing yet. It really doesn't make sense for her to test before her dad or me. Her dad also has a history of breast and ovarian cancer in his family. This increases the chances of my daughter having received a BRCA gene mutation that could lead her to cancer diagnosis.

I can't stand the thought.

Danielle's Story

I was 11 years old when my mother died of ovarian cancer. It was a very sad and uncertain time for me. I understood that cancer was a disease and that the kind of cancer my mother had was very serious and often fatal. I remember thinking at the time of her illness, and for years after her death, that I would probably get cancer too. This thought did not bother me because even though my mother died of cancer I did not believe that cancer would kill me.

When I was 26 years old I started to think about cancer more because information was becoming available about cancer genetics. I was told that the BRCA1 gene mutation had recently been identified in my family. After genetic counseling, I agreed to have genetic testing. I wanted to know if I also carried the gene mutation and thought this information would lead me to be more conscientious in screening for breast and ovarian cancer.

I was not frightened at the possibility of testing positive for the gene mutation. I felt that knowing my status would put me in a good situation. I figured that if my test rendered a negative result - great! Less worries about increased risk and what I would do to prevent getting cancer. And I thought that a positive result would allow me to make informed decisions to be more proactive in managing the increased cancer risk.

I tested positive for the BRCA1 gene mutation and I had two concerns. The first, was that I was hoping to have at least one more child, so I increased my cancer screening (mammogram and pelvic ultrasound). And the second concern was - what should I allow my doctor to put in my medical charts? Now that I think about it, I think it's pretty sad that after being told that I had a 60 - 80 percent chance of being diagnosed with ovarian or breast cancer one day, all I could think about was what would the insurance company do if they found out? I lived in the United States and so health insurance coverage was foremost in my mind due to publicity that raised the issue that insurance companies could refuse coverage or increase premiums based on genetic test results or information.

My oldest sister had already made her decision to have preventive surgery removing her breasts, and ovaries and was very happy to be rid of the fear of such a high risk of cancer. I felt time was running out for me. In our family, the cancer usually showed up in the early thirties. I decided with my doctor's urging to put my BRCA1 gene status and my family history of cancer in my medical charts. My doctor was great and promised that he would fight in court if need be so that genetic discrimination would not be an issue. This relieved me greatly. My husband's insurance book stated that the insurance would pay for prophylactic surgery for patients with strong family history of cancer. So, finally I had to decide which was more important: to have another child regardless of how long it would take to get pregnant or to continue living with the fear of an impending cancer diagnosis. I wanted to reduce my risk as much as possible; and I had two young sons already.

This was a hard decision. I had thoughts of getting pregnant and not having breasts to feed my baby, something I loved being able to do for my two boys. I wondered how I would look with implants? People had said they might shift… what did that mean? Would my husband still find me desirable? Would I recover fast? Would I continue to have the same range of motion in my arms? And how would our boys deal with me after the surgery? I had no family close by to help out if I needed help.

After considering my situation and dilemma I decided to have the double mastectomy first, and if another baby was in my future, I could feed the baby by bottle - as many people do.

One year later, the implants look great, and there is no shifting or moving. My husband loves the bigger size (and so do I)! I have very realistic nipples made from the skin of my inner thigh that is naturally darker and gives the illusion of "real" areolas.

My neighbors made two weeks worth of prepared dinners and were great support. The boys (ages 3 and 6) were also good, being careful not to jump on me, although to this day I have to remind them to be careful where they plant their elbows.

The biggest upside is that I have a very low breast cancer risk, and this is totally worth the sacrifice of having little to no feeling in my breasts and slight rippling on my upper breasts.

I gave up my dream of having more than two children and agreed to reduce my risk for ovarian cancer by having a total hysterectomy. I consoled myself by admitting that if God thought I was ready to have more children he would have given them to me by now, and I want to live for the children I have and not worry about a high risk for ovarian cancer and dying before they are grown up.

For my peace of mind these prophylactic surgeries were the right choice for me. I no longer feel that I am likely to be diagnosed the familial cancer. I have changed my body in order to keep it healthier and to give me a greater chance of living into old age. It was a roller coaster ride of emotions with fear and hope all tangled up. But now, my hope for the future is bright.

Nancy's Story

I discovered that I had inherited a gene mutation that increases my risk of developing, not only breast, but also ovarian cancer to a level that is so high, I get chills when I think about it. The fact that I carry this BRCA2 gene mutation is now as much a part of my personal identity as is my age, my religion (Jewish), and my educational training (Masters in Public Health). I have been married to the same wonderful, supportive man for more than 30 years. We have a son and a daughter, both of whom have a 50 percent chance of having inherited this mutation. They have not had gene testing yet, but they intend to do so. I have one sister who has chosen not to have children. I've worked in the health field all my life and despite my family history and my educational training, I had no idea what a profound effect the discovery of my mutation would have, not only on me, but on my nuclear and extended family.

My family is very small, and cancer has always been a part of its history. Three of my four grandparents and both of my parents had cancer. I have lived with a terrible fear of developing breast cancer, since 1980, when my mother was diagnosed with it at the age of 58. She died just five months later. Remembering the agony of watching her die is like trying to remove a pen mark from a piece of paper. It made an emotional imprint on me that can never be erased. In my mind, breast cancer became a disease that could never be survived.

Although I inherited my fear from my mother, she may not have been the parent who gave me this mutation. She may have been one of those unlucky one out of eight women who develop post-menopausal breast cancer. I inherited this mutation from my father. Seven years ago, when he was 76, he was diagnosed with breast cancer and he underwent a mastectomy. Until then, I had never given any thought to the fact that men can and do get breast cancer. After his surgery, my sister and I became very concerned about the breast cancer legacy our parents have given us. My sister learned about a breast cancer family research study, into which she entered our father.

The day before Christmas in 1996, a genetic counselor from the study called to tell my sister that a BRCA2 gene mutation had been discovered in our father, and that we, his children each had a 50/50 chance of having inherited it. I was alone in my house when my sister called to tell me. I will never forget the words she chose: "Nancy, I have something to tell you that you won't like." My immediate reaction to this news was that I wanted to know my genetic status. I could not imagine not knowing information as important as this. I am certain that somewhere deep inside of me, I knew I would have a double mastectomy if I too, tested positive.

Our respective physicians felt that this specialized field of medicine was beyond their level of expertise. Therefore, my sister and I were referred to genetic counseling programs at our local hospitals. We went through the same counseling process simultaneously in different cities. During my first counseling appointment, we covered an incredible amount of material in a two hour education only session. I was very appreciative, and more so retrospectively, that neither the nurse nor the genetic counselor biased the discussion with their own personal feelings. On the way home, I told my husband, who was by my side at every doctor appointment, that if one of us were to test positive for our father's mutation, I felt that I had better coping skills than my sister.

It is very common for programs not to allow patients to have their blood drawn at that first counseling visit because it is believed that we need time to process the vast amount of information we receive at that time. As I look back, I am very grateful for that. I needed time to process the implications of this information for my life and my future. I even considered what I saw as a real dilemma: what if I should test negative? I would be removed from the risk of developing hereditary breast cancer, but I could still be the one out of eight women who will develop what they call sporadic breast cancer. I was so convinced I would develop it some day that I considered that testing positive might be a relief.

I made the appointment for my blood draw about four weeks after my initial counseling session, and about four weeks later, the results were ready. I was not particularly anxious during this waiting period, but my anxiety level soared when they called to postpone my results appointment. My sister's good news had been ready in three weeks. She tested negative.

I had an ominous feeling as the nurse talked about the weather during that long walk from the lobby to the conference room. I wanted her to cut to the chase so I said, "Just tell me if it is good or bad." When the genetic counselor answered my question directly and said, "It's bad," I had a visceral reaction. It was as if someone had punched me.

I had no idea my life would become permanently altered that day in March 1997 when the genetic counselor announced that I had inherited the breast cancer gene mutation. Knowing my family history of breast cancer had already created a fear in me, the depths of which, I think are truly understood only by those who share similar histories. I had always felt that it was a question of when, not if, I would get breast cancer, and knowing I had this gene mutation only heightened my fears. I'd been told that my lifetime risk of developing breast cancer was between 50 - 80 percent, but for me, that lifetime risk felt like a daily risk. I could not focus on anything but this time bomb living inside me. Every day when I got dressed, I wondered, "Is this the day that I'll find the lump?" But the worst part was that I felt so alone. I had not anticipated how difficult it was to live with this new information about myself. What made it more difficult for me was that not one of my friends was there for me. It was a very isolating time. Most people consider only two groups – those with breast cancer and those without it. To my friends, because I didn't have a diagnosis of breast cancer, I was simply in the healthy people group. To me, however, I was one small step away from those with breast cancer, and it was only a matter of time before I would be joining them.

I wanted nothing more than to talk to someone who was in my situation, but my condition was unique, and there was no place for me to turn. At the time, I was the only patient who did not have cancer who had tested at the genetic counseling center. All the other women who sought genetic counseling and testing had already been diagnosed with cancer. Their reasons for testing were different from mine. Most had the testing because of their additional concern for their children. I tested primarily because of concern for my health. I thought about joining a breast cancer support group, but something in my gut told me it was wrong. My plastic surgeon validated my intuition by explaining there is a definite pecking order among women with breast cancer. I fall at the very bottom. I was so afraid of opening myself up to displaced anger of women with conditions far more serious than mine that I decided against joining a support group. So instead, I lived in isolation.

I decided after about one month, I had to do something to lower my risk of getting breast cancer. There are really three choices available to those of us who carry a breast cancer gene mutation: 1) careful and constant monitoring, including frequent breast exams and mammograms, 2) chemoprevention (Tamoxifen), and 3) preventive surgery – to have our breasts removed. On my own, I investigated Tamoxifen, but decided against it because of potentially risky side effects. Then I went back to my surgeon, hoping for some reassurance about the option to carefully monitor my breasts. First, she showed my mammogram to me. My breasts were large, very dense, and cystic. She told me that if I were to get breast cancer in this part of one breast, or that part of the other breast, it would never show up on mammography. It became apparent that there was no reliable method of monitoring and early detection for me. I asked her what she would do in my position. She replied that she and I might react differently, so what she would choose might not be right for me. However, her next sentence was the one that influenced me. She said, "You must balance the anxiety you have about living with the possibility of developing breast cancer with your fears of disfigurement." I knew then, a preventive mastectomy was my only choice. The surgery would not totally eliminate my risk, because the surgeon could not remove every breast cell, but it would reduce it to a level that seemed acceptable.

There is a tremendous amount of fear swirling around the subject of genetic testing. Many people believe if our genetic status is revealed to employers or insurance carriers, our futures will be jeopardized. Although I was aware of these issues, I decided that to improve my chances of even having a future, I would move forward with the surgery and not worry about these possibilities. My health insurance paid for the testing – no questions asked. They also agreed to pay for the mastectomy. However, when I requested coverage for breast reconstruction, their agreement came only after some debate. After all, they argued, I didn't have breast cancer and my surgery wasn't medically necessary, so why should they have to pay?

Some managed-care issues resulted in a several-month delay in scheduling my surgery. I spent those months grieving and crying. I didn't need anyone else's validation that I had made the right decision, even though people frequently assumed that's what I needed. What I really needed during that time, and almost never got, was acknowledgment that the primary issue in my life was that I was living with a paralyzing fear related to this gene mutation. I discovered that people with chronic disease and women with breast cancer learn through sharing with others in similar situations. I am now in a new, different, and permanent place in my life, and only those who are there with me can really understand what I am going through.

This new information affected not only my nuclear family and me, but also rippled its way across the country to extended family members. All the women that my sister told supported my decision for preventive surgery. However, very few of the men did—including her husband—who happens to be a physician. He kept telling me that they have made great technological advances in early breast cancer detection. I finally said to him, "Phillip, I know that I'll get breast cancer some day. I'm doing this so I don't have to do chemo and radiation, and I get to keep my lymph nodes." He finally got it.

I spent the evening before surgery crying in my husband's arms. One of my worst fears, and one that I could find no one to talk to about, was what this loss would mean for our sex life. I knew I wouldn't find out until it was too late, and I was terrified. I was also terrified of what they might find when they did the tissue pathology. What if I was too late and they found a malignancy?

I will never forget how surreal everything felt the morning of my mastectomy. I decided that even if I wasn't going to enjoy my day, my surgeon should at least enjoy hers, so I drew a sad face on my breasts with Mercurochrome before I left for the hospital. The surgery went smoothly. However, I felt let down by a couple of people during my hospitalization – my surgeon who promised, but forgot, to order a Reach to Recovery volunteer to come and visit me; and the oncology nurse who told me that I didn't need her because I didn't have cancer.

Although I was uncomfortable post-operatively, I was surprised by the lack of pain. I had visions of spending my first post-operative week in bed crying over the loss of my breasts, but I think the relief of reducing my breast cancer risk not only neutralized the fears that had haunted me before surgery, but also allowed me to postpone dealing with my grief for several weeks, until I began to feel better physically.

The grief did surface however, and I found myself depressed for many months after my surgery. I realized I was not only grieving for my breasts and the life I used to live, but also reevaluating my priorities like many women with breast cancer do. Rather than allowing me to "get on with my life," as I had naïvely thought it would, my surgery became a catalyst for several unexpected life changes. The most notable was, after recognizing that my re-prioritized values did not match the values of my corporate employer, I accepted a significant salary reduction when I left my job to take one that felt more meaningful to me. While I was happier personally and professionally, that change in our financial status was accompanied by a surge of guilt that I was not doing my part in helping to pay our daughter's hefty college tuition bills.

Since my surgery, two comments have emerged consistently from almost everyone who knows me. The first is that my decision must have been a very difficult one. However, to me, there was no decision. I inherited this gene mutation and mammography might not detect a malignancy, so for me, surgery was my only option. The second comment was, "You are so brave." For several months, my response was, "I feel far from brave. I am scared." But as time has passed, I've learned to give myself credit and recognize that I was brave in the way I faced what has been a life crisis for me. Fear can do one of two things to people - it can be a great motivator or it can paralyze them. For me, it served as a call to action.

During the three years after surgery, I had three more surgeries: shoulder surgery, breast reconstruction, and a total abdominal hysterectomy to remove the ovaries, further reducing my risk of developing ovarian cancer. While the risk of getting ovarian cancer for women with this gene mutation is lower than the risk of getting breast cancer, early detection of ovarian cancer is almost impossible. It is most likely that my father's mother died of ovarian cancer, so I never hesitated to have this final surgery. I realized earlier that I had to bring closure to my breasts before I could allow myself to lose another body part. All three surgeries were difficult in their own ways. Not a day goes by that my body fails to remind me what I have put it through. After each surgery, I found myself dealing with an overwhelming and unexpected loneliness. I think in my friends' minds, none of the surgeries stirred up their concern like my mastectomy did, and after that, they were just not as supportive as they had been before. Each surgery was another frightening reminder of how this gene mutation has affected my life.

Even after all of this time, I find I am dealing with a few issues and dilemmas I have yet to resolve. The most difficult of all is that I constantly question if I am a breast cancer survivor or not. I have undergone more disfiguring surgery than many women who have been diagnosed with breast cancer.

I have been unable to participate in the Race for the Cure since my mastectomy because I still don't know where I belong – with the survivors or with their supporters. I also struggle to determine if and when it might be appropriate to share my new identity with new acquaintances. While I don't want it to define relationships, it certainly has defined my life, and I struggle to balance the two.

For those of us who have lost mothers to breast cancer, we are different in many ways from patients whose mothers have survived the disease. We have another issue to grapple. If we did not finish grieving for our mothers when they died, and I did not, chances are that this grief will reappear. At each step of this journey, I found myself revisiting and grieving separate, yet intertwined losses.

Another issue that weighs heavily is this – where will I find the strength to guide and support my children through their journeys related to genetic status? I hope that some day they will follow through and discover whether or not they have inherited this gene mutation. The ultimate paradox I've been trying to reconcile is that it seems absurd to me that my father might have feelings of guilt for having passed this gene mutation on to me, and yet, guilt is the only emotion I feel when I consider that I may have also passed this legacy on to my son or daughter.

Then, the subject I know everyone is reluctant to discuss – the sexual one. I will tell you bluntly that I have lost a very erogenous part of my body. I have yet to come to terms with the sadness I feel about this loss and how it has affected my sex life. While I was trying to adjust to this loss after my surgery, I realized nobody ever talked about it with me – not one of my doctors and none of my friends.

I must admit I have done something I never thought possible while I was in the acute phase of my crisis – I have found and recognized the positive that has resulted from this experience. First, I have gained invaluable insight and understanding about life, loss, and sadness that no other experience could have afforded me.

I speak to other women, on this path, and offer support and validation of their fears in the way that I wish someone had for me.

My surgery has freed me from the constant anxiety I had of developing breast cancer. I have come to recognize that breast cancer is not a condition you either have or don't have. It is truly a continuum, and gene testing has made it possible for some of us to learn that we are farther along on that continuum than we realized. I realize I have reacted to my situation in a very personal way, and not all high-risk women would make the same choices I have. Not all women want this information about themselves. A relatively small number of women who think they do, decide after genetic counseling, not to go through with testing as I did, and that's okay. We need more research and dialog in this area, because gene testing for susceptibility to breast and ovarian cancer is just the beginning of what we'll be able to test for 10 years from now.

I am confident about what I have done and have never wished I had made different choices. My pathology report validated my choice. Analysis of the breast tissue revealed no cancer but did locate a benign tumor that should have been but was not detected on the mammogram I had just four days before my surgery. The pathologist's report also documented cell changes that precede breast cancer. Given what I have gone through I can't thank the scientific community enough for having provided me with the information that led me down this path. To me, ignorance is NOT bliss.

Suzanne's Story

I knew that my grandmother had breast cancer and her mother had died of cancer, so when my sister was diagnosed with breast cancer, I was not overly surprised. At the time, I was a social worker working with people who were unable to work due to serious illness or permanent disability. The week my sister was diagnosed, one of my clients was a terminally ill lady with breast cancer. The week she died, I was diagnosed with breast cancer. I got a new job.

Due to my sister's diagnosis, and our family history, gene testing was initiated. The technicians found a mutation on the BRCA2 gene which was different from any they had seen before. They contacted labs throughout the world to find another, but no one else carried the same mutation as the one found in our family. I also tested positive for this gene mutation. My mother was then tested and she carried the gene mutation as well. One of my brothers tested positive, and the other opted not to be tested.

I have two daughters who will have to decide what they want to do regarding gene testing. One is resistant and the other is eager. We will have to consider life insurance and many other things before testing, and after. Cancer has not affected members in our family until after age 40. My sister was 42 and I was 44.

My cancer was caught very early and I had two lumpectomies. My doctor asked what was I going to do when it recurred. He felt that the risk for a recurrence was very high based on the identified gene mutation and my family history. At that time, I felt that I had entered the "hurry up and wait" stage of life. Decisions had to be made, only to be followed by long waits before anything could be acted upon.

My initial diagnosis and lumpectomies happened in February and I was at the cancer clinic at the end of March for follow up.

Religious by nature, I could not pray. I did not know what to pray for – for strength to handle death well or the will to fight the great fight. I finally prayed to know what I should pray for and when a song came on the radio that went in part, "I want to stand with you on a mountain, I want to stand with you by the sea," I knew that I needed to fight. Peace came over me once I made that decision.

My husband and I felt that the stress of having mammograms and waiting for a recurrence was not an option, so we decided that I would have preventive bilateral mastectomies and TRAM flap reconstructive surgery. I was glad I made that decision because the biopsies showed extensive precancerous ductal carcinomas.

My husband took time off work to be with me after the surgery. What impressed on my mind is that cancer affects everyone in the household. I believe that it's easier to be the one fighting than to be the other family members who watch and wait. I now have more patience, faith, and a more balanced perspective about my family.

It has been six years since my diagnosis and I have no cancer. I know that I can't be complacent, as precancerous lesions have been removed from my bowel, another site this gene mutation imposes on. I am active, work, and keep busy with my family. I will be there for them as they face genetic counseling. Many friends, and friends of friends, have had cancer since my journey started and I now have an understanding of what they are facing.

Yes, I have had, and continue to have a great life. I tell my girls that I plan to live to 97!

Author's Epilogue, Monique Achtman

Since I've been through gene testing and prophylactic surgery, I have been sharing my story. It is a story that begs to be heard. From acquaintances to strangers, from friends to close family, the interest does not wane. Even doctors want to know how I'm doing as time goes on.

Some of the people I meet wonder how I have the courage to share such a personal story, and how I can be so willing to "show and tell" what is normally considered so private – my breasts. I have come to the conclusion that in some situations, my breasts do not represent a private, intimate part of me at all. While I still experience a sense of intimacy about my breasts in my relationship with my husband, my health care journey and chosen role as health care advocate have given me a new ease and public confidence in my body.

A rough comparison can be made to a woman waiting in hospital to give birth. Doctors, nurses and interns frequently check the progress of her dilation. Her sense of modesty is soon replaced by a more urgent need to have a healthy delivery. I too now have a more urgent need – to demonstrate the possibility of taking steps to greatly lower cancer risk. The trade-off for me was a good one – less breast sensation for the chance at a longer life. And the results for me have been amazing – beautiful firm reconstructed breasts that look and feel natural, and a renewed optimism that I will live to raise my children and meet their children.

When I initially started to tell the story to families of cancer survivors, they would exclaim, "You should write a book!" Months later, they would inquire, "How's the book coming along?" I'm glad to tell them that the book is finally complete. I can now share my story with many more women, men and families who may be considering hereditary breast and ovarian cancer gene testing. I am happy to share this personal story, to show that our physical and psychological needs are every bit as important as our need for life itself.

Life is more than just a destination; it's a journey, and my journey continues...

APPENDIX B

Affirmations

I developed these affirmations to help determine when I was ready to consider genetic counseling and testing:

- I am starting off with a positive mental attitude to be proactive about my health.
- I am finding out all that I can about my family health history, particularly in the area of cancer genetics.
- I am willing to discuss my health concerns with my family.
- My doctor is aware of my family history and health concerns.
- I have a doctor who is aware of the latest research on cancer genetics.
- My doctor will give me a high risk cancer surveillance plan incorporating mammograms, clinical breast exams, the CA-125 and pelvic and transvaginal ultrasounds.
- My doctor will be in contact with my genetic counselor and other professionals working with me.
- I make a list of questions to ask my doctor.
- I am willing to consider anything that I can do to reduce my genetic cancer risk.
- I appreciate the sacrifices others made so I can receive counseling and gene testing when I'm ready.
- I eat a well-balanced diet and exercise regularly.

- I have a strong support group of family and friends.

- I know I am going to do my best to reduce my inherited cancer risk, if there is one.

- I have pleasant activities planned for whenever I may become depressed.

- I have goals to achieve and projects to complete as I look forward to the future.

APPENDIX

C

Making the Decision to be Tested

Other considerations must be carefully evaluated before agreeing to gene testing. The genetic counselor will guide you through these types of questions:

- Are you living in fear of a cancer diagnosis that occurred with a family member?
- Do you have any living cancer survivors in the family?
- Would they consider having gene testing?
- Has a gene mutation been identified in your family?
- How long are you prepared to wait for the results of gene testing?
- Who would you want to have access to your test results?
- Do you have life insurance? Could you be discriminated against because of genetic test results?
- Would the identity of a gene mutation in your family affect your employment?
- Will your health care plan meet your expectations, i.e. paying for genetic counseling, gene testing and subsequent treatment?
- Are you prepared to share this information with your family (spouse, parents, aunts, uncles, cousins, siblings, nieces, nephews, and your own children)?
- What might their reactions be?

- If your siblings obtain their test results and test differently from you, could your relationships change? If so, how?
- What plan of action will you follow if the result is positive for a cancer gene mutation?
- What plan of action will you follow if the result is negative for a cancer gene mutation?
- Is cancer gene testing really important for you? Why or why not?

APPENDIX

D

Internet Support

Having lost my mother to cancer at a young age, I have lived with a nagging fear of being next in line. This fear has, at times, seemed as overwhelming as what it would be like to live with a cancer diagnosis. At first, it was difficult to find others like me, who had not been diagnosed with cancer but were considering cancer treatment to reduce the risk ahead of time. I searched the Internet and found a breast cancer newsgroup, where most had been diagnosed with breast cancer, while some were concerned family and friends of cancer survivors.

I joined Breast Cancer Listserv (an e-mail bulletin board of messages) and queried the list of approximately 1,000 breast cancer survivors about the idea of gene testing. Within hours, I received several replies warning me not to reveal that I was considering gene testing in such a public forum. I was told that even though the users were registered, privacy issues were still a big concern. People said insurance companies and others could be lurking and sifting through the information. Some felt that their personal information could lead to denial of health and life insurance, and possible employment opportunities. I didn't understand how individuals or companies could take my information from e-mail and use it against me. However, the issues were raised and we do have to be careful about how much information we share via the computer. I appreciated the notes of encouragement I received from the members on the list.

Some of the cancer survivors I corresponded with explained how they dealt with the affects of diagnosis, treatment options, diet and lifestyle changes, and more difficult family dynamics. I asked them if they had ever considered finding out whether their cancer was triggered by a cancer gene mutation or not. In an effort to protect their family, their first response was they didn't even want to think that their loved ones might be at risk. They also expressed a desire and hope to allow their family the right to choose not to know whether a cancer gene mutation might exist in their family. I empathized with the cancer survivor who lamented the fact that she already represents, in a physical way, the risk of occurrence in the family. It was encouraging for me to share in return that as a cancer survivor, she also represents the survival of the family.

Fortunately, a support network of friendship and love has been created on the Internet. It is a very good forum for sharing feelings, thoughts, concerns, and conflicting opinions. I asked questions and received answers more quickly than possible from anywhere in the world. What a special blessing to have made such important friends and to have been fortunate enough to meet a few in real-life. I asked questions about life before and after breast cancer and before and after breast reconstructive surgery. After reading the posted messages and "meeting" some of the breast cancer survivors, I shared concerns about my potential risk factor.

One of the most important questions I asked was, "If you knew that you had a 100 percent chance of developing breast cancer, and were given the option to have prophylactic surgery before it developed, would you do it to be spared the absolute cancer diagnosis that you have received?" I e-mailed this question to the list of breast cancer survivors and received about forty replies. Only a few of those who replied were against the preventive surgery, suggesting instead, I watch my diet and exercise and not worry so much about something that might or might not happen. They also added assurance that a breast cancer diagnosis is certainly not the worst thing in the world to happen to a person. They shared many examples of how they felt their lives have been enriched in many ways as a breast cancer survivor. Their cancer diagnoses eventually allowed them an opportunity to know themselves better, become more independent, and more empowered to be free to grasp a new vision of their mortality. Some said they did not know whether they would go back to being cancer free if they had to give up the good friendships, support, and self-esteem gained since their diagnosis. I was awestruck by their sincerity and how strong they were to have overcome the fear of cancer and to have been able to grasp a new life more fully than the one they had before.

When I read the other replies, the authors considered my situation and said that given the opportunity, they would have chosen prophylactic surgery in a heartbeat. They urged me to avoid, at any cost:

1) Cancer diagnosis. This totally throws your world into immediate confusion and chaos. It challenges your relationships, your self-value, and your will to live, at least at the beginning.

2) Chemotherapy. It is the worst treatment in so many ways, yet it is offered as one of the most powerful treatments to save your life and help you combat the disease. Some added that losing their hair after chemotherapy was worse than losing their breasts or ovaries.

3) Radiation. No one I communicated with liked radiation. They all encouraged me to do anything I could to avoid diagnosis that might lead me to radiation therapy.

4) Recurrence. I was also told that cancer survivors live in fear of recurrence elsewhere in the body and not to underestimate the fact cancer treatment is still not a cure.

With these words of encouragement and poignant, honest concerns that breast cancer survivors deal with so well, I decided to undergo gene testing. At that time, I decided that if testing determined I had inherited a BRCA1 gene mutation, I would request prophylactic surgery of my ovaries, and perhaps, my breasts too.

APPENDIX

E

Recommended Reading & Resources

Recommended Reading

A Woman's Decision: Breast Care, Treatment and Reconstruction
by Karen J. Berger and John Bostwick, III

Assess Your True Risk of Breast Cancer
by Patricia T. Kelly, Ph.D.

Breakthrough: The Race to Find the Breast Cancer Gene
by Kevin Davies and Michael White

The Breast Reconstruction Guidebook: Issues and Answers from Research to Recovery
by Kathy Steligo

Motherless Daughters: The Legacy of Loss
by Hope Edelman

Letters from Motherless Daughters: Words of Courage, Grief, and Healing
by Hope Edelman

Resources in Canada

Alberta Cancer Genetics Program
Web site: https://www.acgp.ca/

Canadian Association of Genetic Counselors
Web site: http://www.cagc-accg.ca

Canadian Breast Cancer Network
Web site: http://www.cbcn.ca/
Tel: 1-800-685-8820
The Canadian Breast Cancer Network (CBCN) is the national voice of breast cancer survivors and serves as the pulse of Canada's breast cancer community.

Canadian Breast Cancer Research Alliance
790 Bay Street, Suite 1000, Toronto, ON M5G 1N8
Web site: http://www.breast.cancer.ca/
E-mail: cbcra@cbcf.org
Tel: (416) 596-6598
Fax: (416) 596-1714

Canadian Cancer Society
Web site: http://www.ontario.cancer.ca/
E-mail: info@cis.cancer.ca
Tel: 1-888-939-3333
This Web site will give you information about hereditary breast cancer. Audio tapes and printed booklets are also available.

Hereditary Breast and Ovarian Cancer Society of Alberta (HBOC)
E-mail: hboc.society@shaw.ca
Tel: (780) 920-5591
The Hereditary Breast and Ovarian Society of Alberta is a provincial non-profit organization dedicated to promoting education and support to individuals, families and communities impacted by hereditary breast and ovarian cancer.

National Ovarian Cancer Association (Canada)
27 Park Road, Toronto, ON M4W 2N2
Web site: http://www.ovariancanada.org/
E-mail: noca@ovariancanada.org
Tel: 416-962-2700 or 1-877-413-7970 (toll free)
Fax: 416-962-2701
The National Ovarian Cancer Association is dedicated to overcoming ovarian cancer, providing leadership by supporting women and their families living with the disease, raising awareness in the general public and with health care professionals, and funding research to develop reliable early detection techniques, improved treatments and ultimately, a cure.

National Cancer Institute of Canada
10 Alcorn Avenue, Suite 200, Toronto, ON M4V 3B1
Web site: http://www.ncic.cancer.ca
Tel: (416) 961-7223
Fax: (416) 961-4189

Ovarian Cancer Alliance of Canada
Web site: http://www.ocac.ca/
Tel: (604) 877-6187
Provides a voice for Canadians in all regions who have been touched by Ovarian Cancer; to mobilize support for improved diagnosis, treatment and outcomes for Ovarian Cancer; and nationwide access to information regarding Ovarian Cancer.

Resources in the United States

American Board of Genetic Counseling
9650 Rockville Pike, Bethesda, MD 20814-3998
Web site: http://www.abgc.net/
Tel: (301) 634-7316
Fax: (301) 634-7320

Cancer Genetics Network
Web site: http://epi.grants.cancer.gov/CGN/
Cancer control and population sciences. A resource supporting the research community at large.

Myriad Laboratories
320 Wakara Way, Salt Lake City, UT 84108
Web site: http://www.myriad.com
Tel: 1-800-469-7423 (Patient and Health Care Info.)
Fax: (301) 634-7320

FORCE: Facing Our Risk of Cancer Empowered
16057 Tampa Palms Blvd. W., PMB #373, Tampa, FL 33647
Web site : http://www.facingourrisk.org
Tel: (954) 255-8732
Fax: (954) 827-2200
Provides women with resources to determine whether they are at high risk for breast and ovarian cancer due to genetic predisposition, family history, or other factors. Information is available for families investigating options for managing and living with breast and ovarian cancer high risk factors. This group represents the concerns and interests of our high-risk constituency to the cancer advocacy community, the scientific and medical community, the legislative community, and the general public.

National Cancer Institute
Web site: http://www.nci.nih.gov/
NCI Public Inquiries Office
6116 Executive Boulevard, Room 3036A, Bethesda, MD 20892-8322
Tel: 1-800-4-CANCER (1-800-422-6237) or TTY: 1-800-332-8615

National Society of Genetic Counselors
233 Canterbury Drive, Wallingford, PA 19086-6617
Web site: http://www.nsgc.org
E-mail: FYI@nsgc.org
Tel: (610) 872-7608

R.A. Bloch Cancer Foundation, Inc.
4400 Main Street, Kansas City, MO 64111
Web site: http://www.blochcancer.org
Tel: 816-WE BUILD (816-932-8453), 1-800-433-0464
Fax: (816) 931-7486

APPENDIX

F

Glossary

Amniocentesis
A diagnostic test used to determine the health of an unborn baby. This test can detect a number of genetic and chromosomal abnormalities (such as Down's syndrome) in the fetus. It is also helpful in diagnosis of lung maturity, and neural tube defects (such as spina bifida).

Ashkenazi
A Hebrew term referring to people of eastern European Jewish heritage, primarily from Germany, Poland, and Russia, as opposed to the Sephardic Jewish people coming primarily from Spain, France, Italy, and North Africa.

Autogenous Breast Reconstruction
The use of your own body's tissue to reconstruct the breast. This includes the TRAM (transverse rectus abdominus myocutaneous flap), Gluteal Flap (gluteus maximus myocutaneous flap), latissimus dorsi flap, DIEP (deep inferior epigastric perforator flap), SIEA (superficial inferior epigastric artery flap) and GAP (gluteal artery perforator flap) techniques.

Bi-lateral Mastectomy
Surgical removal of breast tissue from both breasts.

BRCA
BReast CAncer genes associated with inherited breast cancer syndrome.

BRCA Gene
Tumor suppressor gene, which every human being carries.

BRCA1 Gene Mutation
Pertains to breast and ovarian cancer risk, and an increased risk of prostate cancer as well as male breast cancer.

BRCA2 Gene Mutation
Pertains to breast and ovarian cancer risk in females; and in males, prostate cancer, and a higher male breast cancer risk than with the BRCA1 gene mutation.

BRCA3
A term that is symbolic for BRCA gene mutations yet to be identified.

Breast Cancer Surveillance
Testing methods for early breast cancer diagnosis; mammography, breast self-examination, and clinical breast examination.

CA-125 (Cancer antigen 125)
CA-125 is a protein found at levels in most ovarian cancer cells that are higher than normal cells. The CA-125 test assesses the concentration of CA-125 in the blood. The test should be part of a cancer surveillance plan including transvaginal ultrasound, and pelvic examination.

Characteristic
A distinguishing mark or quality.

Chemoprevention
Natural or laboratory-made cancer drugs (e.g. Tamoxifen) used to prevent cancer. The people who participate in chemoprevention trials are healthy or are at risk of developing cancer.

Chromosome
Structure found in the cell nucleus which contains genetic material (DNA). Humans have 23 pairs of chromosomes, one of each pair is inherited from the mother and one from the father. Each chromosome contains hundreds or thousands of genes that make up our genetic blueprint.

Colon
Large intestine or bowel located between the small intestine and the rectum.

Colonoscopy
Examination of the lining of the colon (large bowel) using a long, narrow flexible tube which is inserted into the anus.

Confidential
Held private, or secret. Pertains to what information can be shared with others in the family, or other organizations by your health care provider.

Consent
Verbal or written agreement.

Deletion
A particular kind of mutation: loss of a piece of DNA from a chromosome. Missing a gene or part of a gene can lead to a disease or abnormality.

Diagnosis
To identify or determine the cause of a situation or problem (diagnose).

DIEP Flap
DIEP is an acronym for Deep Inferior Epigastric Perforator. This is the named vessel for transferring tissue in breast reconstructive surgery. "Flap" is a plastic surgery term referring to the donor tissue.

DNA (Deoxyribonucleic Acid)
The substance that contains genetic material found in chromosomes in the cell nucleus. The genetic instructions contained in DNA are needed to build a living being and for the day to day activities of each body cell, such as growth, development and replication.

Ethnic
Member of a race or people distinguished by their cultural, religious or linguistic characteristics.

Exon
A DNA molecule that contains coding information for a protein.

Expert Medical Opinion
An opinion based on personal experience of a medical specialist.

Free-flap TRAM (Transverse Rectus Abdominus Myocutaneous)
A surgical procedure where a plastic surgeon uses a body's own muscle, skin, and tissue to reconstruct a breast following mastectomy.

Gene
A sequence of DNA. Genes are the coded instructions that determine our genetic make-up such as eye or hair color.

Gene Expression
The process by which proteins are made from the instructions encoded in DNA.

Gene Mutation
A permanent change or alteration in a gene that causes a disruption of function. It is this disruption that predisposes individuals with a BRCA1 or BRCA2 mutation to develop cancer.

Gene Testing
The examination of a DNA sample, to identify significant differences or mutations in the gene.

Generation
People grouped according to relationships as parents and children; average difference in age between parents and offspring of about 25 years.

Genetic Counseling
Information and discussion about inherited or genetic factors.

Genetic Counselor
Professional counselor specializing in discussing genetic risk and management issues with patients. Most genetic counselors have a scientific background.

Genetic Discrimination
According to the *Human Genome Program* of the U.S. Department of Energy, genetic discrimination is "prejudice against those who have or are likely to develop an inherited disorder."

Genetic or Hereditary Predisposition (re: developing cancer)
An increased tendency towards developing cancer, based on the information of a strong family history and/or from gene testing.

Genetic Surveillance
Identifying people at risk of developing a specific disease or of passing such a disease on to their children.

Geneticist (see medical geneticist)

Genetics
The branch of biology that deals with heredity; study of genes within the DNA on the chromosomes.

HBOC
Hereditary breast and ovarian cancer. HBOC affects 1 in 500 people in the general population; varies with ethnic groups; affects 25% of women diagnosed with breast or ovarian cancer under age 50. Breast, ovarian, prostate, and colon cancer are part of the known HBOC syndrome.

Hereditary
To inherit, transmitted from a parent to a child.

Hysterectomy
Surgical removal of the uterus. Also see Total Hysterectomy.

Implant Reconstruction
Breast reconstruction using saline or silicone implants. This type of reconstruction tends to require a few operations before a final result is achieved. Usually performed on patients who don't have enough donor tissue to use in autogenous breast reconstruction.

Inherit
To receive genetic characteristics by heredity.

Lumpectomy
Surgical removal of a cancerous lump from the breast.

Lupus Erythematosus
An inflammatory disease of the skin giving rise to scaly red patches, especially on the face, and sometimes involving internal organs.

Malignant
The ability of cancer cells to invade and spread.

Mammogram
A photograph of the breasts made by X-rays.

Mastectomy
Surgical removal of breast tissue from one or both breasts.

Medical Geneticist
A medical specialist involved with the study of genetics.

Metastasis
Transfer of cancer from one part of the body to another through the blood stream or lymphatics.

Mutation
A change in the DNA sequence that alters the function of a gene.

Neonatologist
A medical specialist on the diseases and care of newborn babies.

Oncologist
A medical specialist who studies the development, diagnosis, treatment and prevention of cancerous tumors.

Oophorectomy
Surgical removal of an ovary (bilateral oophorectomy - removal of both ovaries).

Ovary
Tissue in females that contains the eggs or ova.

Pelvis
Bony hip girdle located at the base of the spine and resting on top of the legs - contains the contents of the lower abdomen.

Penetrance
To do with how likely it is that a gene mutation will cause a cancer to develop.

Predictive Test
Examination of the genes for specific mutations to assess if the patient is carrying a gene mutation that makes them much more likely to develop cancer than others in the general population.

Predisposition
Susceptibility.

Preventive or Prophylactic
Taking action to prevent a possible outcome, such as having surgery to prevent cancer occurring.

Prophylactic
Preventing disease.

Prostate
Glandular tissue located at the base of the bladder in men.

Prosthetic
Artificial implant – e.g. silicone breast implant; or special brassiere (bra) that incorporates two pockets to hold the artificial breasts.

Protein
Organic compound made out of amino acids.

Reconstructive Surgery
Plastic surgery that restores or creates a natural look to the breasts after a mastectomy using saline or silicone implants or donor tissue from the patient's body. Also see Free-flap TRAM or DIEP.

Renal
Pertaining to the kidneys.

Surveillance
To examine closely or keep watch.

Susceptibility
Capable of being changed, influenced or easily affected.

Syndrome
Pattern of symptoms or features that characterize a disease or condition.

Total Hysterectomy
Removal of the uterus, ovaries and cervix.

TRAM
Transverse Rectus Abdominus Myocutaneous. The use of one's own body's tissue to reconstruct the breast.

Transvaginal Ultrasound
Test performed via the vagina to get the best visualization of the ovaries.

Tumor
Abnormal swelling or mass of tissue independently in the body with no physiological function, may be benign (non-cancerous) or malignant (cancer).

Tumor Marker
An antigen that provides a measurement of tumor activity.

Tumor Suppressor Gene
A gene that helps prevent the transformation of normal cells into cancer cells. When both copies of a tumor suppressor gene are mutated in a cell, the lack of suppression may lead to the development of cancer.

Ultrasound
A probe is used to measure high-frequency sound waves off the body and create an image of the tissue inside the body.

NOTE: A more comprehensive glossary of genetic terms can be found at http://www.genome.gov/glossary.cfm

APPENDIX G

Biography

Monique Achtman was born in Calgary, Alberta, Canada. At age 15, she started selling church bulletin advertising with her mother and was encouraged to own and operate her own business from that time on. In 1987, she joined the Calgary Entrepreneur's Association and met her husband, Myron. They have two children.

Monique speaks to different groups and organizations, among them, cancer patients and concerned individuals via telephone support (Bloch Cancer Help Line), and online at the FORCE Web site (www.facingourrisk.org). She has been the subject of articles in Mamm Magazine and The Calgary Herald. She has appeared on the Dave Rutherford Show on QR77 Radio, CBC Radio, and was featured on CFCN Television with Barb Higgins, Buddies for Life, 2000.

Web site: http://www.aminextinline.com

Memberships
Hereditary Breast and Ovarian Cancer Society, Edmonton, Canada.
Independent Book Publishers of Canada (IPAC) Calgary, Canada.

Other books written by Monique Achtman
The Special Care Baby Book, a keepsake journal for parents of premature babies with extended hospital stays after birth. To order, call 1-800-668-0102.

How to Publish a Home-Based Business Directory, a business opportunity to increase awareness of home-based businesses in your community. To order, call 1-800-668-0102.